THE BEGINNER'S GUIDE TO USING TAX LISTS

BY CORNELIUS CARROLL

CLEARFIELD

Originally published
Harold, Kentucky, 1996

Reprinted for
Clearfield Company, Inc. by
Genealogical Publishing Co., Inc.
Baltimore, Maryland
1997, 1998, 1999, 2000, 2002

International Standard Book Number: 0-8063-4707-4

Made in the United States of America

A comprehensive and indepth study of the tax records, records associated with them, and the various and sundry laws governing the tax records of each colony, territory, and state, and time period, is beyond the scope of this book. A project of this type would require endless hours of research and a format far larger than the current one. I hope the small contribution this book makes to expanding the knowledge of what tax records are and how they can be used will enable genealogists who are just beginning their family research to better understand how to document their line and will open a new field of research for experienced genealogists which may answer many of their questions. Commonsense and documentation are the basic keys to sound research. I make no claims to being an expert on the subject, but I believe this book will help genealogists learn what I have learned on my own over the years. I take full credit for any mistakes made herein.

I would like to express my thanks to Connie Maddox and Pikeville College for their permission to use abstracts from the book Carry Me Back in the historical sections of this book.

"TAX LISTS ARE ONE OF THE MOST VALUABLE, BUT ALSO ONE OF THE MOST NEGLECTED SOURCES OF GENEALOGICAL AND HISTORICAL INFORMATION. THEY CAN NOT ONLY BE USED TO TRACE THE MIGRATION ROUTES OF ANCESTORS, BUT THEY CAN OFTEN BE USED TO PROVE PARENTAGE, BIRTH DATES, AND DEATH DATES. THERE ARE ALSO MANY OTHER USES THAT MANY GENEALOGISTS DO NOT EVEN SUSPECT. THIS BOOK HAS BEEN COMPILED TO HELP RESEARCHERS AND HISTORIANS LEARN TO USE TAX RECORDS TO UNLOCK VALUABLE INFORMATION."

TABLE OF CONTENTS

CORNELIUS CARROLL
3 CLARK BRANCH
HAROLD, KY 41635-9601

CHAPTER ONE: RECORDS AND RULES

Tax lists are one of the most valuable, but most neglected sources of genealogical and historical information. They can not only be used to trace migration and determine the taxable property of ancestors, but they are also important because they can be used to prove parentage when no other records are available. There are also many other uses which many genealogists and historians do not suspect.

It is important to understand the provisions and statutes that apply to the tax lists you are researching, but even without an indepth knowledge researchers can learn valuable information. The laws concerning the ages and classes of people who were tithable will vary from state to state and from one time period to another.

Due to the fact so many of the surviving tax lists are fragmentary and large numbers have been lost or destroyed, your ancestor may unfortunately only appear in the years for which they are missing. Tax lists are not a cure-all, but they do provide an excellent source of information. They, along with other census substitutes, allow researchers to bridge gaps many genealogists think are untraceable.

Tax lists basically consist of the heads of households, males of 16 (or the prescribed age), slaves (male and female), cattle, horses, other types of personal property, land taxes, and notes of interest. Sometimes land and personal property tax lists are combined. And heads of households were expected to pay a county or parish tax on all free males between the ages of 16 and 21 years. Some older individuals may still remember the poll tax that was paid earlier this century.

• •

In 1607 Jamestown was established and became the first permanent colony in what is now the United States. "There were about 104 colonists on the first three ships to land at Jamestown. But only one of them had any descendants! Many of the immigrants who came in the first few years died of disease, starvation, or Indian arrows. Of the 900 persons who had come to Virginia, only 150 were alive at the end of 1609. And in the terrible "starving time" of that winter, more than half of them died!"[2]

The massacre of 1622 almost wiped the colony out. The reputation Virginia gained caused some English prisoners to choose to be hanged instead of emigrating to the colony.

Much can be learned about the early immigrants by studying the census returns, parish registers, passenger lists, and militia rolls.

WHAT ARE TAX LISTS?

Tax lists is a term used to describe personal property tax lists, tithables, poll lists, land tax lists, and rent rolls. They place individuals in a particular place at a particular time and indicate the amount and type of property owned. They also indicate the relationship of individuals in a household and their approximate ages.

Tax lists are often the only source of documentation that an individual lived in an area during a particular time period.

[2] Bluegrass Roots, Vol. 23, No. 1, Spring 1996, p. 12.

4

QUIT RENTS

The 1704 Quit Rent Rolls of VA are considered the first "census" of VA by genealogists. Quit rents were a yearly tax based on the amount of acres owned, payable directly to the Crown; they were customary fees due for taking out land grants. Only the rolls for 1704 have been found. These rolls are for the counties that used the "headright" system, not the Northern Neck counties, between the Potomac and Rappahanock Rivers, who paid quit rents to the Lords Proprietors, the Fairfax-Culpepper family.

In the Northern Neck the headright system was never recognized. In order to acquire land a person had to purchase a warrant and obtain a survey before they were issued a grant.

"The headright system was in operation in 1618 and became more and more important until it was the principal basis for title to land. Every London Company shareholder who transported a person to Virginia, bond or free, received a claim to fifty acres if the person remained in Virginia three years, or even if he died on the outward voyage. Each shareholder secured an additional tract of fifty acres in the second distribution of lands upon the strength of the transportation of these persons. Even then acquisition by headright was not confined to shareholders. Anyone who immigrated to the colony, or who brought or sent over another was entitled to fifty acres."[2] "Title to all the land in Virginia was vested in the King who granted it to the London Company in the sea-to-sea charter of 1609. During the time of the Company, the Colonists held the land either through bills of adventure or by headrights."[3]

"When the Company was dissolved, there was much apprehension expressed by the Colonists concerning the legality of land titles. But at the dissolution the Crown confirmed all the land grants made by the London Company. After 1624 the Governor and Council were empowered to give land patents, which did not have to be returned to England for confirmation."

"When a person received a grant of land, an article in the patent provided that he was to receive a due share of all mines and minerals found on his property. This was in addition to the common feudal privileges of hunting, hawking, fishing, and fowling, which every landholder exercised on his own grant. For every one hundred acres held the grantee paid two shillings a year quit rent, which was to be paid in specie. However, when specie was difficult to provide, which was true most of the time, the rent was paid in tobacco or some other merchantable commodity. Each year the sheriffs in the counties made an "exact" roll of all the lands held in Virginia. The purpose of the roll was to acquaint the Governor and Council with the status of landholders in the colony and to prevent any attempts to evade the quit rent. Despite the repeated requests of the governors for an exact rent roll, the first complete and accurate one was not taken until 1704. At the time the sheriffs made the rent roll they were ordered to report any waste of land being committed on plantations. Waste included the unnecessary felling of timber, land lying idle with no good cause, failure to tend the crops and animals, dilapidated and unsafe buildings, general improvidence, and failure to seat land within the allotted time."[o]

[2] Carry Me Back, p. 125.
[3] Ibid., p. 129.
[o] Ibid., p. 130.

"Conferring a patent prompted the recipient to carry out two very important conditions which had to be met before the title was perfected. Failure to comply resulted in forfeiture. Seating and paying the quit rent were the two conditions. Seating consisted of building some kind of dwelling, having a small stock of cattle roam the woods, and planting one acre of tobacco or corn. This condition had to be fulfilled within three years after the grant was made. By a law of 1618, all persons who received their land through headrights were required to pay twelve pence for every fifty acres held. The charge varied somewhat through the years, but in any case it was not to go into operation until seven years after the land had been patented."
"Owners of plantations along the unprotected frontier had additional conditions to meet. No frontier plantation could be seated without four able hands well-armed, according to a dictum by the Assembly in 1664."[2]
A list for the five counties in the Northern Neck of VA for 1704 has been compiled from the land grants of the Proprietors of the Northern Neck of Virginia.

WHO WAS TITHABLE?

Since this book deals primarily with the tax records of VA and KY, I have included a brief discussion of the laws governing tithables. These laws were originally abstracted from Hening's The Statutes At Large by Landon C. Bell for his book Sunlight On The Southside. For more detailed information on these and other acts, check the corresponding volumes.
Using the 1704 Quit Rent Rolls as a starting point, the following laws provide the essential information researchers need:

The act of Oct. 1705 provided: "'That all male persons, of the age of sixteen years, and upwards, and all negro, mulatto, and Indian women, of the age of sixteen years, and upward, not being free, shall be, and are hereby declared to be tithable, or chargeable, for defraying the public, county, and parish charges, in this her majesty's colony and dominion; excepting such only, as the county court and vestry, for reasons, in charity, made to appear to them, shall think fit to excuse.'"
"The governor and his family and 'beneficed ministers' within the colony were exempted from the operation of the law."[3]
By an act of May 1723, it was enacted : "'That all free negroes, mulattoes, or Indians (except tributary Indians to this government) male and female, above the age of sixteen years, and all wives of such negroes, mulattos, or Indians (except before excepted) shall be deemed and accounted tithables; any law, custom, or usage, to the contrary, in any wise, notwithstanding.'"[o]
By the act of 1738, "mariners and seafaring persons, not freeholders, commonly employed in navigation, and who out of their wages paid 'toward the support of Greenwich Hospital' were 'exempted from being listed as tithables'."[¶]
In Oct. 1748, "an act was passed covering the subject of tithables, and repealing the above noticed acts." "This law defined tithables as 'all male persons of the age of sixteen years and upwards, and all

[2] Carry Me Back, p. 130, 131.
[3] Sunlight On The Southside, p. 42, 44.
[o] Ibid., p. 44.
[¶] Ibid., p. 44.

negroe, mulatto, and Indian women of the same age, except Indians tributary to this government and all wives of free negroes, mulattoes, and Indians, except before excepted,' and 'excepting such only as the county courts, for charitable reasons appearing to them, shall think fit to excuse.'"

"The law exempted the governor and his domestic servants, the president, masters, scholars, and domestic servants of William and Mary College, beneficed ministers, and constables, while in office."[2]

"After the foregoing act no law has been noted changing the definition of tithables until 1777."

"The act of Oct., 1777, provided among other things a tax of 'five shillings per poll upon all tithables above the age of twenty-one years (except soldiers, sailers, parish poor, and such as receive an annual allowance in consideration of wounds or injuries received in public service, except also slaves and mulatto servants to thirty-one years of age, who, being property, are rated ad valorem as aforesaid.'"

"This act provided a tax of ten shillings for every hundred pounds value on 'all manors, messuages, lands, and tenments, slaves, mulatto servants to thirty-one years of age, horses, mules, and plate,' etc."[3]

"An act of May, 1779, abandoned the plan of taxing slaves on a valuation, and provided for the taxing of them as polls. It provides 'That a tax of five pounds per poll shall be paid for all negro and mulatto servants and slaves' except those who through old age or bodily infirmity were incapable of labor."

"There seemed to be no express provision for a minimum age for slaves in order to be taxable under this law."[o]

"In May, 1780, a law was enacted reverting to the plan of 1777 of taxing slaves on the basis of valuation instead of per poll. This act, respecting tithables provided for a tax as follows: 'for every white male tithable above the age of twenty-one years' there 'shall be paid three pounds six shillings and eight pence (except the officers of the line or navy, soldiers or sailers in the service of this commonwealth or of the United States, or persons disabled in such service; except also such of the militia who may be in actual service at the time when the said taxes shall respectively become due, and those who have been or shall be exempted from the payment of levies by the county court;) for every white servant whatsoever, except apprentices under the age of twenty-one years,' there 'shall be paid the like tax.'"[¶]

"In Nov., 1781, the legislature passed an act for establishing a permanent revenue. One of the provisions of it was for a tax of ten shillings on 'every free male person, above the age of twenty-one years, who shall be a citizen of this commonwealth, and also upon all slaves, to be paid by the owners thereof, except such free persons and slaves as shall be exempted on applications to the respective county courts through age or infirmity.'"[®]

"A similar provision was contained in an act passed in Oct., 1782, and this law required 'every master or owner of a family' to annually give in his list of 'the names of all free male persons above the age of twenty-one years, and the names, and numbers of slaves, distinguishing those that are tithable,' etc."[•]

[2] Sunlight On The Southside, p. 45.
[3] Ibid., p. 46.
[o] Ibid., p. 46.
[¶] Ibid., p. 46.
[®] Ibid., p. 46, 47.
[•] Ibid., p. 47.

"During the Revolutionary period, and thereafter, largely as a consequence of it, various and sundry tax laws were passed. Considerable uncertainty and confusion resulted respecting many provisions of these laws. One such law, that of May, 1783, it seems, must have been deemed to raise a question respecting the taxation of tithes. In consequence of this a later act in the same year, among other things provided: 'That nothing in said act contained, shall be construed to prevent the several county courts from causing lists to be taken of all free male tithables, between the ages of sixteen and twenty-one years, and of imposing taxes upon all such for the purpose of county or parish levies.'"[2]

In Oct., 1786, the Virginia Assembly passed a law which mandated that tax commissioners should "on the tenth day of March annually, begin and continue proceeding without delay through their respective district, and call on every person subject to taxation or having property in his or her possession for a written list thereof...make four alphabetical general lists therefrom, showing in columns according to the form hereto annexed, the date when each list was received, the persons chargeable with the tax or taxes, and the number or quantity of every species of property, inserting particularly the names of all free males subject to tax, distinguishing those also subject only to parish and county levy."[3] Prior to this act, the tax commissioners had set up offices with residents of their districts "delivering, or causing to be delivered" to them a list of their taxable property. This act grouped taxpayers into neighborhoods and made the tax lists especially valuable to genealogists and historians.

STATE CENSUSES

Before the first Federal Census of 1790, there were State Censuses. Many settlers from VA had already immigrated to NC prior to and during the period the State Censuses were taken (and prior to their migration to TN, then KY). In order to cast some light on the NC connections of our ancestors, I have used the 1784 State Census of NC as an example.

"At a General Assembly begun and held at New Bern on the Twenty Second of October, in the Year of our Lord One Thousand Seven Hundred and Eighty-Four, and in the Ninth Year of the Independence of the said State: Being the First Session of this Assembly, Alexander Martin, Esq. Governor."

"Whereas it is recommended by the United States in Congress assembled, that the number of white and black inhabitants, and free citizens of every age, sex and condition, including those bound to servitude for a term of years, and three-fifths of all other persons not comprehended in the foregoing description shall be taken in each State; and in order to comply with the above recommendation."

"...That the several county courts in this State, shall within six months after the passing of this Act, appoint a proper person in each captain's district to take a list of the number of white and black inhabitants and free citizens of every age, sex and condition in each district which list shall distinguish the number of blacks from whites and other free inhabitants in the following manner: White males from twenty-one years old to sixty, White males under twenty-one years old and above sixty, White females of every age, Blacks of each sex from

[2] Sunlight On The Southside, p. 47.
[3] The Statutes At Large, Vol. 12, p. 246.

twelve to fifty, Blacks upwards fifty and under twelve years old. And the lits by them so taken, shall be returned to the court which shall sit next after their appointment, which lists shall by the clerk of the court be immediately transmitted to the Governor...and by him sent to our delegates at Congress."

"And if any master or mistress of a family, his or her agent, director, manager, or attorney, after due notice given by advertisement of the same at the most public place of the district, shall fail to give in a list of his or her family, as by this Act required, he or she so failing or neglecting, shall forfeit and pay the sum of fifty pounds."[2]

"In Virginia, state enumerations were made in 1782, 1783, 1784, and 1785."[3]

THE FIRST (FEDERAL) CENSUS

"The First Census act was passed at the second session of the First Congress, and was signed by President Washington on March 1, 1790. The task of making the first enumeration of inhabitants was placed upon the President. Under this law the marshals of the several judicial districts were required to assertain the number of inhabitants within their respective districts, omitting Indians not taxed, and distinguishing free persons (including those bound to service for a term of years) from all others; the sex and color of free persons; and the number of free males 16 years of age and over."

"The object of the inquiry last mentioned was, undoubtedly, to obtain definite knowledge as to the military and industrial strength of the country."

"By the terms of the First Census law nine months were allowed in which to complete the enumeration. The census taking was supervised by the marshals of the several judicial districts, who employed assistant marshals to act as enumerators."

"The assistant marshals made two copies of the returns; in accordance with the law one copy was posted in the immediate neighborhood for the information of the public, and the other was transmitted to the marshal in charge, to be forwarded to the President."

"The columns are headed as follows: Free white males 16 years and upward, including heads of families. Free white males under 16 years. Free white females, including heads of families. All other free persons. Slaves."[°]

"There were...difficulties which were of serious moment in 1790, but which long ago ceased to be problems in census taking. The inhabitants, having no experience with census taking, imagined that some scheme for increasing taxation was involved, and were inclined to be cautious lest they should reveal too much of their own affairs. There was also opposition to enumeration on religious grounds, a count of inhabitants being regarded by many as a cause of divine displeasure. The boundaries of towns and other minor divisions, and even those of counties, were in many cases unknown or not defined at all."

"In many localities there were no roads, and where these did exist they were poor and frequently impassable; bridges were almost unknown."[¶]

[2] State Census Of North Carolina 1784-87, p. 4.
[3] North Carolina Census - 1790, p. 3.
[°] Ibid., p. 4.
[¶] Ibid.,p. 5.

CHAPTER TWO: HOW TO USE TAX LISTS

One of the most commonly asked questions is "What can tax lists be used for?" In this section of the book, I will attempt to answer the above question.

PARENTAGE, BIRTH DATES, AND DEATH DATES

Outside of a family Bible, there are few ways that you can prove the age of an individual. Tax lists are one of the most accurate ways. Many individuals never even knew their birth date so even pension applications and other court documents may be inaccurate. Ages may vary by as much as ten to twenty years in census records and the census dates and information were not always turned in by the head of the household or a member of the family.

Many people couldn't read or write and county officals signed their names for them and they made their identifying mark. The identifying mark is essential when tracking individuals with common names through deeds and court records. Even the ones who could write often spelled their name in different ways. The English language also underwent changes over time.

"Until the reign of Queen Anne the English language was extremely variable and unsettled. The best informed men, writing of the same period, would spell the same words very differently."[2] (Queen Anne was the second daughter of King James and reigned from 1702-1714. She was the last monarch of the House of Stewart.)

The tendency to consistently spell ones name the same way is a modern phenomenon. Tax lists, like all court records, must be checked for every possible variant spelling of a name. For example; Robertson may be spelled Roberson or Robinson. Names were more often than not spelled the way the person listening heard them (phonetically). Names were also anglicized (the French names Reynau became Reno and Chaumette became Shumate) and shortened (Fitzgerald became Gerald, Garrell, and Jarrell). The handwriting of incompetent or indifferent clerks and tax commissioners also adds to the confusion.

On the early frontier, there were few schools and illiteracy was widespread. The problems confronting census takers can be illustrated by an amusing but true story from a more recent time. During the early 1900's, a census taker was visiting the head of one of the branches on Big Mud Creek, Floyd Co., KY. He ask the housewife when one of her children was born and she replied "At blackberry picking time." He ask about another child and she replied "When Duz's cow had a calf." This points out how dates were often marked by events rather than actual dates on a calendar.

An additional problem occurs once you have found a birth date. By 1582 the accumulated error in the Julian Calendar was estimated to amount to 10 days. "In that year Pope Gregory XIII decreed that the day following Oct. 4, 1582, should be called Oct. 15, thus dropping 10 days and initiating what became known as the Gregorian Calendar." Most of Europe had adopted the calendar by 1700. "The British government imposed the Gregorian Calendar on all its possessions, including the American colonies, in 1752. The British decreed that the day following

[2] The Quit Rents Of Virginia, preface.

Sept. 2, 1752, should be called Sept. 14, a loss of 11 days. All dates preceding were marked O.S., for Old Style. In addition, New Year's Day was moved to Jan. 1 from March 25 (e.g., under the old reckoning, March 24, 1700 had been followed by March 25, 1701). George Washington's birthdate, which was Feb. 11, 1731 O.S., became Feb. 22, 1732, New Style (N.S.)."[2]

The process for determining the parentage of an individual is simple. A male became tithable when he reached 16 (or the prescribed age). Some lists only have the number of males tithable in a household, but many list the sons by name. Even if the males are not listed by name, you can sometimes determine the parent by following the tax lists until the males appear in their own households.

Pittsylvania Co., VA Tax Lists

1767 - William Mullins & William Mullins Jr.   2 tithes
1773 - William Mullins & John Mullins   2 tithes
       William Mullins Jr.   1 tithe
1774 - William Mullins, John, & Ambrose   3 tithes
       William Mullins Jr.   1 tithe
1775 - William Mullins Sr. & Ambrose   2 tithes
       William Mullins Jr.   1 tithe
       John Mullins   1 tithe

The above tax lists provide strong circumstantial evidence that William Mullins Sr. was the father of William Jr., John, and Ambrose Mullins. (It can usually be assumed a male in the household with the same surname is a son.) The lists also provide approximate birth dates: William Jr. ca 1751 (at least 16 in 1767), John ca 1754, and Ambrose ca 1758.

In his Revolutionary War pension application of 30 Jan. 1835, Ambrose Mullins states "I was born in Franklin County, State of Virginia in the year 1751 to the best of my recollection and information." When ask if he had any record of his age, he replied "I have none, nor never had any." Ambrose was born in the part of Pittsylvania County that later became Franklin County, but the 1774 tax list indicates he was approximately 7 years younger than he stated in the application.

There are some tax lists that leave no doubt as to the relationship of the tithables in a household.

Pittsylvania Co., VA Tax Lists

1773 - Samuel Hall and son Thomas   2 tithes
1774 - Samuel Hall and son Thomas (1 slave)   3 tithes

Why some tax commissioners chose to use this detailed information in their districts or for certain households is unknown, but we are fortunate they did.

It should also be pointed out that because two individuals in a district have the same surname it does not mean they are related. This is especially important to remember when you are working in an area and time period where the tax records are fragmentary or the lists for certain years are missing.

Always follow the lists year by year! As an example:

[2] The World Almanac And Book Of Facts 1995, p. 288.

Pittsylvania Co., VA Tax Lists

1768, 1769 - Missing
1770 - Henry Mullins
1771, 1772 - Missing
1773 - Henry Mullins & Thomas West   2 tithes
      Peter Mullins   1 tithe
      Matthew Mullins   1 tithe

Pittsylvania was formed from Halifax Co. in 1767. The only complete tax lists for the years between 1767 and 1773 are the ones for 1767 and 1773. The 1770 tax list is fragmentary and neither William Mullins Sr. nor his son William Jr. appear on the surviving portion. Henry Mullins does appear on the list. In 1773, Henry, Peter, and Matthew Mullins appear on the tax list as does William Mullins Sr. and William Mullins Jr.

Since the tax records are incomplete, you cannot automatically assume Henry, Peter, and Matthew were sons of William Mullins Sr. In fact, other records show Henry Mullins emigrated to the area ca 1770.

Tax lists in which males became tithable at 16 are much more useful than the lists in which males became tithable at 21. The reason is simple. Most males were already married and in their own households by the time they were 21. Thus, research with tax lists where males were tithable at 21 is much more difficult and must be substantiated by other records when possible. If only one family with the surname lived in the area, it is fairly simple to note the males as they appear in their own households on the tax lists, but you must constantly be aware of the possibility that another family with the same surname may also appear in the area unexpectedly. It will often require research in the deed, survey, and court order books to seperate the two families and establish the exact location where each family lived and the districts they would be taxable in.

The penalities for failure to report a tithable were severe. The act of Oct. 1705 provided: "'That the owner or purchaser of every child, being a servant, and the parent or importer of every child, being free, at the first, second or third court, held for the county where such child shall be, after the arrival of the said child in this country, shall bring the said child before the county court, to have its age adjudged by the court; otherwise the said child to be accounted, and thereafter immediately become tithable as aforesaid, although not of the age of sixteen years; And the age of such child being adjudged by the court, shall be entered upon the records of the said court; and be accounted, deemed and taken, for the true age of the said child, in order to its becoming tithable, within the intent and meaning of this act.'"

"Another provision of this act was: 'That the court of each county, divide the same into convenient precincts, and to annually appoint one of the justices of each of the said precincts, to take a list of tithables; every which justice, in convenient time, before the tenth of June then next following, shall give notice of his being appointed thereto, and of the place he designs to take the same at, by setting up note thereof, at the church or chapel door of the precinct he is appointed for; and shall attend the same, on the said tenth day of June, if it happen not to be of a Sunday, and then on the next day following. And also in August court the next following, shall deliver the list so by him taken, together with the subscriptions of the tithables, to the clerk of the county court; who shall, the next court day, set fair lists thereof, up in the court-house, there to remain during that sitting of the court, for the view and inspection of all that please, and for the discovery of such as shall be concealed.'"

"This law provided: 'That every master or mistress of a family, or in his or her absence, or non-residence at the plantation, his or her attorney or overseer, shall, on the said tenth day of June, by a list under his or her hand, deliver, or cause to be delivered, to the justice appointed to take the same, the names and number of all the tithable persons abiding in, or belonging to, his or her family, the ninth of June, or the master or owner thereof, shall be adjudged a concealer, and be liable as a concealer of such and so many tithables as shall not be listed and given in; and for every tithable person so concealed, or not given in, and listed, as afore is directed, shall forfeit and pay one thousand pounds of tobacco to the informer; to be recovered, with cost, by action of debt, bill, plaint, or information, in any court of record in this her majesty's colony and dominion wherein no essoin, protection or wager of law shall be allowed. And if any justice appointed to take the list of tithables, shall not truly enter and list the names and number of his own tithables in that district, in the list he gives in, he shall be adjudged a concealer; and for every tithable person so by him concealed, and not listed, shall forfeit and pay one thousand pound of tobacco, to the use aforesaid; and to be recovered, with costs as aforesaid, in manner and form aforesaid.'"[2]

An act of November 1738 "indicates that there were tax dodgers in those early days. It recited that some persons owning plantations in different counties and parishes 'when they have known, or been apprehensive that the levies would run high in one of those counties, or parishes, by reason of public buildings, or other emergencies' had been known 'to remove their tithables, some small time before the ninth of June, out of the said county, or parish, to some other plantation in another county, or parish; and afterwards, in a short time' return them 'to the county, or parish, from whence they were so removed.' The act provided that any person so doing should be adjudged a concealer, and liable to penalties and forfeitures provided by law for that offense."[3]

The penalties for concealing tithables or other taxable property were updated and changed over the years. The following court cases illustrate how the law worked and the results of the court action.

Washington Co., VA Court Order Books

20 Nov. 1782. "Martin Duncan makes information upon oath that James Alley Senior has concealed of his Taxable property (to wit) ten head of horses, ten head of cattle and two Tithables."

18 Feb. 1783. "Ordered that the prosecution against James Alley be dismissed and that Scirefacias issued against James Alley Junior and Peter Alley."

18 March 1783. "Be it remembered that James Alley Senior, Thomas Alley and Christopher Cooper are bound to the commonwealth in the sum of Fifty pounds that is to say the said James Alley in the sum of twenty five pounds and each of his securities in the sum of twelve pounds ten shillings of their respective goods and chattels and Land to be levied

[2] Sunlight On The Southside, p. 42, 43.
[3] Sunlight On The Southside, p. 43.

and to the said commonwealth rendered yet upon this condition that the said James Alley be of good behavior to all people of this commonwealth and particularly to Martin Duncan then this obligation to be void else to remain in full force and virtue."

2 May 1783. "Martin Duncan against James Alley > In trespass assault & Battery. By consent of the parties all matters in difference are mutually submitted to the determination of Patrick Porter, William Robinson, Andrew Davis, George Dailey, and Bazil Baron and their award to be made the Judgement of this Court and the same is ordered accordingly."

The death date of the male head of a household or males in the household can be determined by their disappearance from the tax lists. The widow will usually be listed in the first tax list following her husband's death along with her taxable property and tithables, but she will not be tithable. There are exceptions to the rule and every possibility must be checked out. The male head of a household may have left the county after he and his wife seperated or he may have been away at the time the list was taken and his wife will be listed as the head of the household. This is especially true during the time of "The Long Hunters" and during war when men were often away from home for two or more years and the wives never even knew if they were still alive. And sometimes the husbands were erroneously reported to be dead.
An example of the lengthy period of time that could pass before the final fate of a family member was known is shown by the Revolutionary War pension application of John Mullins, dated 26th May 1823, Floyd Co., KY: "He enlisted in the service of the United States against the common enemy in the year 1779 for a term of three years under the command of Capt. Henry Conway, who was a captain in the 1st Virginia Regiment, commanded by Col. Ball in the Virginia Line of Continental Establishment, and that he was in the following battles; The Battle of Stoney Point and in the Battle at the seige of Charlestown in South Carolina, which was about two years after his enlistment, and was at the Battle at the seige of Charlestown taken a prisoner of war by the British and was by the British taken a prisoner of war to England and there kept until peace was made. He further states that he never had it in his power to return to America for 11 years..."
It is much harder to determine the death date of the female head of a household. Depending on her age, there are a number of reasons why she may disappear from the tax lists: she may have died, she may have remarried and left an older son as the head of the household, she and the children may be living with the stepfather or with relatives, the oldest son may be listed as the head of the household instead of her, or she may have left the county.
In later census records, it must pointed out that some women who listed themselves as widows were never married and their children were illegitimate.
There are some tax records that leave no doubt as to whether the head of the household was a widow, but you will often have to trace widows by the disappearance of their husbands from the tax lists.

Ann Brown (the widow of Israel Brown)   1 tithable, 600 acres of land

The lists also sometimes mention heirs by name. By checking the court order books, you can verify birth and death dates.

Floyd Co., KY Court Order Books

25 Oct. 1808. "John Hatfield, deceased, is exonerated from the payment of the levy of 1807 out of his estate."

28 Feb. 1809. "Ordered that Sarah Brown be exempted from payment of the levy of 1807 for her son John, deceased."

23 Oct. 1809. "Patsy Hatfield improperly listed her son Samuel as a tithable for the levy of 1808. Ordered son exempted."

FREE NEGRO, MULATTO, AND INDIAN ANCESTRY

As stated in the previous chapter; Free Negroes, Mulattoes, and Indians (except tributary Indians) male and female, above sixteen years, and all wives of such Negroes, Mulattoes, and Indians were tithable.

The following information has been abstracted from Carry Me Back, Slavery And Servitude In 17th Century Virginia by Dr. Robert S. Cope. I highly recommend this book to anyone who is interested in a factual history of the subject. As the author points out, Virginia was the third colony to legalize slavery not the first. The first two colonies were Massachusetts in 1641 and Connecticut in 1650.

"According to John Smith, the first Negroes were introduced into Virginia in 1619. His account says, 'About the last of August (1619) came in a Dutch man of Warre that sold us twenty negars'. Whether these first Negroes were servants or slaves is still a question which has not been settled."[2]

The component parts of the free Negro class "was composed of the following groups: (1) children born of free colored parents; (2) mulatto children born of free colored mothers; (3) mulatto children born of white servants or free women; (4) manumitted slaves (most important); (5) mulatto children born before 1662."[3]

"In Virginia the three general methods by which slaves were manumitted or legally set free were as follows: (1) by act of legislature; (2) by the last will and testament of the master; (3) by deed."[o]

"Contrary to twentieth century opinion, there was a close bond between many of the masters and slaves in sevententh century Virginia. This fact is born out in the deeds of manumission. It was the custom and later the law of indented servitude in Virginia that the servant, white or colored, should receive "freedom dues" from his master at the time of discharge from service. Following this procedure nearly all the seventeenth century wills of manumission contained grants of property to freed Negroes. Frequently the master gave the emancipated slave certain commodities for his own comfort and benefit in addition to the freedom dues."[¶]

Freedom could also be achieved "through the purchase of their papers by a person who would then free them."[®]

"In some instances the color element operated in favor of the Negro. An interesting fact pertaining to the massacre of 1622 is that not one Negro was killed during the most devastating Indian uprising in the

[2] Carry Me Back, p. 5.
[3] Ibid., p. 31.
[o] Ibid., p. 32.
[¶] Ibid., p. 35.
[®] Ibid., p. 36, 37.

history of Virginia."[2]

"The last year in which it was possible for a Negro to come to Virginia as a servant and to acquire freedom after a limited term of service was 1682."[3]

"The first land grant to a free Negro was made in 1651 to Anthony Johnson of Northampton County. The basis for this patent was the headrights on the importation of five white persons into the colony. In 1654 one hundred acres in Northampton County were granted to Richard Johnson, a Negro, for the importation of two white men. For all intents and purposes the free Negroes who owned land had the same rights and privileges in regard to their land as had the white people. Free Negroes owning property could transfer it by deed or transmit it by will as was the custom. Land so held remained in their possession or in the possession of their descendants."[°]

Some free Negroes "were highly regarded by both the white people and by the Negro slaves...and were considered for public office." This "was probably responsible for the restrictive act by the Virginia Assembly in 1705, which stipulated that no Negro, mulatto, or Indian was capable of holding any office or place of public trust. Any Negro, mulatto, or Indian who held such a position was to pay five hundred pounds sterling plus twenty pounds a month for each month in office."[¶]

"The free Negro usually paid a higher poll tax then the white man. A question arose as to whether free Negro women should be exempted from poll taxes as were the English women. A law of 1668 specified that they should not be admitted to the same exemption as the English, and, therefore, the Negro women were still liable to pay taxes."

"White women and children under 16 were exempt from working in the ground, which also exempted them from taxes. Some masters who wanted to reward Negro women exempted them from working in the fields."[®]

"Since the free Negroes possessed many of the same rights as white persons, some of them felt that it was their privilege to own white servants. This probably was the basis for an act passed in October, 1705, whereby no Negro, mulatto, or Indian, even if Christian, Jew, Moor, or Turk, should purchase any Christian servant. The above mentioned categories could purchase servants of their own race, but if any of them did purchase a Christian servant, that servant was declared to be free. If any person having Christian servants should marry a Negro, Indian, Jew, Moor, or Turk, the servants were to be free. The act of 1705 was merely a reenactment of an earlier law passed in 1670 by which free Negroes were forbidden to own white servants or slaves. However, not before 1832 were free Negroes forbidden to own Negro slaves."[•]

Mulatto children were designated by the law of 1662 as the same race as their mother. "If the mother was a Negro slave, the child became the property of the owner of the mother. If the mother was a white woman, the child would be freed after a term of indenture."[£]

"That the free Negro, mulatto, or Indian had the authority to vote prior to 1723 is demonstrated by the law of that year stating that none of the above mentioned races should thereafter be allowed to cast the

[2] Carry Me Back, p. 15.
[3] Ibid., p. 14.
[°] Ibid., p. 37.
[¶] Ibid., p. 38.
[®] Ibid., p. 39.
[•] Ibid., p. 38, 39.
[£] Ibid., p. 40.

16

ballot."[2]

As the free Negro and slave population increased the laws became more restrictive.

Free Negro, mulatto, and Indian ancestry can be determined by the same methods as white ancestry, but, in order to determine if an ancestor was mulatto or Indian, it is necessary to check all available tax lists because they may only be noted as such in one or two of the lists. Tax lists are often the only source for documenting mulatto and Indian ancestry.

"Census takers were specifically instructed to 'make the enumeration by actual inquiry at every dwelling house or by personal inquiry of the head of every family, and not otherwise;' furthermore, the completed data were to be shown to the informants for additions and corrections. However, errors were common, and an analysis of the 1860 returns in a slave-owning parish in Louisana concluded that 5% of the racial designations were wrong; 23 well-known colored families were listed as white, while 53 families of entirely European origin were labeled "mulatto."[3]

Many census takers based their racial designations on their own subjective judgement of appearance---in contradiction to their stated instructions.

"The U.S. Constitution, which mandated the censuses, also prohibited the enumeration of untaxed Indians." Prior to 1870, "the only racial options for those censused were white, black, or mulatto." Indian was added in 1870. "From the 1700s through 1830 the state of North Carolina defined as mulatto 'individuals with one-eighth Negro or Indian ancestry,' while Tennessee classed as free persons of color 'those whose parent or grandparent was a full-blooded Indian or Negro.'"[o]

Many early settlers of SW VA, E KY, E TN, and W NC have traditions of Indian ancestry. The Sizemore family has a strong, well-documented tradition of Cherokee ancestry.

1748 List taken by Cornelius Cargill - Lunenburg Co., VA

William Joyner	1	James Sizemore	1
William Sizemore	1	Henry Sizemore	1
Ephraim Sizemore	1	Edward Sizemore	1

1750 List taken by Cornelius Cargill - Lunenburg Co., VA

William Joyner, "an old Indian man's list"   1
George Sizemore   1
Ephraim Sizemore   1

The only notation that William Joyner was Indian is the 1750 tax list. George Sizemore was listed next to William Joyner in the tax list so it is possible the Sizemore's and many other families intermarried with these Indian families. If a will or deeds exist for William Joyner, it would be extremely important to check them for the names of his son-in-laws.

Tax lists may help prove the traditions of Indian ancestry and

[2] Carry Me Back, p. 40.
[3] "Slavery In Old Floyd County, KY" by Sherry Shopp Rehr, Old Floyd Co., KY Families, Vol. 1, No. 3, Spring 1996, p. 24.
[o] "Exploring Indian Traditions In Eastern Kentucky" by Sherry Shopp Rehr, Old Floyd Co., KY Families, Vol. 2, No. 1, Fall 1996, p. 27.

pinpoint the period of origin. They may also prove very valuable in tracing the roots of the Melungeon families of E TN and other tri-racial isolate groups.

"The term Melungeon in its anthropological sense" refers to "the interlocking families who moved into, existed in, and dispersed from Hawkins and Hancock Counties, Tennessee."[2] There were a "limited number of Melungeon families in SW VA, NW NC, northeastern TN, and eastern KY" and "fundamentally, in order to be regarded as Melungeon, one had to be a Gibson, Collins, Goins, or Miner, or have married into one of these families. Even then, the social/ethnic category tended to vary with social/economic status."[3]

"The Melungeon families were...intermarried with the famous Sizemore family of the Eastern Cherokee Claims."[3]

According to the Grohse Papers, Vardiman Collins was "probably a half-breed Indian (though some sources describe him as full-blooded) who married Margaret (Peggy) Gibson from Virginia. Known as "Spanish Peggy," she was, in some uncertain degree, of Spanish origin...a sister to Shephard Gibson, who accompanied Vardy Collins in the settlement of Newman's Ridge. ...Grohse estimates they settled all the land from the Virginia State line to Mulberry Gap, between Newman's Ridge and Powell's Mountain." Vardiman, who was from North Carolina, "was the son of Navarah H. (Henry) Collins, who was born in Virginia in approximately 1699" who "was the son of Henry Collins, an indentured servant of Thomas Wood. "Spanish Peggy" was the daughter of John Gibson of Currituck County, North Carolina" who "was the son of Henry Gibson, also of Currituck County who appears on a 1715 tax list for the county. Grohse reports 'the Gibsons were supposed to have been engaged in piracy off the Atlantic coast.'"[°]

"Dr. Christopher Humble, a Presbyterian missionary who visited the Melungeons in early" 1896 "recorded an historical synopsis of Vardy community as he heard it from the local inhabitants. ...As the account goes, the first settlers were Vardy Collins, Shephard Gibson, and Charley Williams. They reportedly emigrated to Tennessee from Virginia or North Carolina and are described as bearing marked Indian resemblances. The Goins, Miners, and Bells, a second group of settlers emigrated from North Carolina, were "'charged (by Whites) with having Negro blood in them'" and "'explained their peculiarities by claiming a Portugese origin.'" And "a later immigration to East Tennessee brought both Jim Mullins," an Englishman who "reportedly married into the Collins family," and "Jim Moore, a British sailor...said to have married a daughter of Charley Williams."[¶]

The first known appearance of "Malungeon" in print was its use "as a slur for "free mixed-blood Indian-Negro" in 1840, Sullivan Co., Tenn., in The Whig newspaper.[®]

The 1755 tax list of Orange Co., NC lists the Collins, Gibson, and Bunch families as mulattoes. Virginia Easley DeMarce states that by the 1740's "the Goins family was...about quadroon or octoroon, but it did have some African ancestry dating to the mid-17th century. In Louisa County, they were closely associated with the Bunch family, which also

[2] "Review Essay: The Melungeons" National Genealogical Soc. Quarterly, Vol. 84, No. 2, June 1996, p. 135.
[3] Letter from Virginia Easley DeMarce, 3 June 1996.
[°] "The Mysterious Melungeons: A Critique of the Mythical Image" by Melanie Lou Sovine, 1992, p. 47, 48.
[¶] Ibid., p. 43.
[®] Ibid., p. 57.

18

had remote African ancestry, but because of economic prosperity was generally treated as white. As for the others, especially Bowling and Collins, I agree with Wes Taukchiray that they were in part a wandering band of Saponi Indians, but I can't prove it yet."[2]

SERVANTS AND SLAVES

"An adequate and stable labor force was indispensable to Virginia. This need remained constant throughout the seventeenth century and was never fulfilled in a satisfactory manner." There were various attempts "made to remedy the situation and to supply the necessary hands to plant, tend, and harvest the important tobacco crops, to clear the forests for new agricultural lands, and to build homes, shops, and factories. Indentured servants, black, red, and white, and slaves, red and black, as well as hired labor were used to improve the economic status of the colony. However, none of them proved the definitive solution to the labor problem."

"The short terms of the indentured servants resulted in a large turnover of workers," but "much that was accomplished was done by the servants, for Negro slavery and the slave trade were of comparatively little importance until the last two decades of the" seventeenth "century."

"Wages demanded by the hired laborers, particularly in the years from 1680 to 1700, were so high that many planters turned to slavery in economic self-defense."

"Negro slavery seemed to offer the planters the stable, tractable labor force required by the tobacco economy of Virginia. The inconvenience of replacing servants whose indenture time had expired was eliminated; clothes and food of inferior quality might be given the Negro; the period of acclamation for the white servant was unnecessary; the master could exercise a stricter system of control over the slave than over the white person; the Negro worked longer and harder than the white person and took a more active interest in the family and plantation. Although the advantages of the slave system given above seem to weight the scales in its favor, the colonists were slow to adopt it as the sole source of the labor supply. In truth, slavery never did completely supplant indentured servitude, for it introduced a social and moral problem which almost defied solution."[3]

"Servitude in Virginia began with the organization of the London Company."¶ "The planters in reality were servants of the" company, "and were to receive a division of the profits and additional land after five years following the first landing. Planters who failed to keep faith as promised received nothing at the time of the division."® "A declaration against the twelve-year rule of the Company...made by a delegation of the colonists revealed that all men had been kept in the colony by force" and "throughout the century in Virginia anyone desirous of leaving the colony had to acquire a license from the governor or at least he had to make known his intention to depart."¶

"Indentured servitude in Virginia operated under a system composed of two forms. One form included all those persons signing articles of indenture in England and were intended for a designated master who paid

---

[2] Letter from Virginia Easley DeMarce, 3 June 1996.
[3] Carry Me Back, p. xi, xii, xiii.
¶ Ibid., p. 53.
® Ibid., p. 50

passage to the colony. These indentures did not necessarily follow a uniform pattern as to the period of indenture or the perquisites involved. ...The period of servitude usually, however, did not exceed seven years. Grouped in the other category were the people who came into Virginia without indentures, but who were obliged to enter servitude to repay the ship captain or merchant with whom they had contracted for their passage. This latter group, upon entering service, were required to serve according to the periods established by the Assembly for the various age groups." The periods varied throughout the century. "This was known as "serving according to custom." Artisans and mechanics sometimes comprised the first group, while ordinary laborers comprised the second."

"The indenture system was established by the Virginia colonists as a protection to both the master and the servant. To the master it guaranteed a certain period of time during which he could expect the servant to assist him in any type of labor. To the servant the indenture guaranteed proper usage at the hands of the master. And at the end of his term the servant could expect certain emoluments which were customarily granted."[2] In 1705 the Assembly changed "custom into law" and "agreed that the masters should accord each servant at the end of his term the following articles: the male servant, ten bushels of Indian corn, thirty shillings in money or the equivalent in goods, one good gun; a female servant, fifteen bushels of Indian corn, forty shilling in money, or the equivalent in goods."[3]

"Property rights early were accorded indentured servants. As a result, some were able to amass considerable estates during the indenture period."[o]

"To prevent" masters "from imposing unwarranted indenture provisions upon servants, the Assembly ordered in December, 1662, that all servants brought in Virginia without indenture and under sixteen years must be taken to the county court to have their ages adjudged within four months from the time they arrived. No contract made between the master and the servant was to be considered legal unless it had been approved by the court."[¶]

The "complaints of servants were quickly acknowledged by colonial authorities who directed faulty masters either to make amends, or to transfer the servant to another employer. In some cases, the servant was freed and the master was ordered to pay him reparations in addition to his freedom."[®]

"The majority of servants arriving in Virginia in the seventeenth century came voluntarily. There was also a brisk trade in servants by the so-called Spirits. The trade was illegitimate, but quite profitable and functioned with the knowledge of English authorities. Spirits were kidnappers who provided cargoes of servants for shipment to Virginia. Motives behind this illicit servant trade were two: first, demand for cheap labor in the colony, and secondly, the profits made by English merchants in vending indentured servants in America."

"Officals in England were content to ship the unemployed and the poor to Virginia and other British colonies in North America because they believed the island to be overpopulated with those two groups. The servant trade to Virginia after 1715 was made up largely of convicts."[•]

[2] Carry Me Back, p. 55.
[3] Ibid., p. 64.
[o] Ibid., p. 95.
[¶] Ibid., p. 61.
[®] Ibid., p. 88.
[•] Ibid., p. 68, 69.

"In March, 1643, the Governor, Council, and the House of Burgesses decided to suspend all processes against colonial debtors incurring debts in England. English creditors suing colonists were prevented from collecting. Not only did the law help the debtor colonists, but when it became common knowledge in England, it seemed to provide debtors a way to escape their creditors. It proved a boon to immigration from England to Virginia."

"The trade in convict servants also developed from the imposition of the death penalty for so many minor offenses in England. There were three hundred crimes punishable by death in seventeenth century England. This penalty sometimes was reduced to transportation to Virginia. Merchants undertook to transport offenders for the money involved and planters accepted convicts for cheap labor. Some colonial governments were anxious to eliminate such importations, and the colonies above Maryland were successful in so doing. As a result, most of the convicts were sent to Virginia and Maryland. Mixed with these criminals were some political prisoners."[2]

"Virginians were apprehensive regarding felons and political prisoners not only because...of the 1663 rebellion, but also because they did not want Virginia advertised as a colony inhabited by lewd and base people. Some of the more influential Virginia planters were responsible for the law prohibiting the introduction of convicts after 1671" which proved to "curtail, but did not halt, the trade in convict servants."

"Even some of the servants complained about the low class of people who came to Virginia as laborers. One of the complainants was Ellen, the servant of Major Hill. She protested that she was one of the few servants who had not come from Newgate or Bridewell. However, according to another witness, she would have been hanged in England if she had not been pregnant. Because of her condition, she was shipped to Virginia as a servant."[3]

"Coming to the colony were large numbers of women from the lower classes in England who tended to be lacking in moral restraint. Contracts under which they were to labor in Virginia discouraged marriage until the terms of indenture had expired."[°] "The maid servants knew they could not get married until their servitude ended, except by the consent of the master. But such consent made the servant free. Few masters therefore would agree to an arrangement of that sort" and "he must also pay for the services of the preacher and clerk, not an inconsiderable amount in itself."[¶]

"The first session of the Assembly in 1619...legislated that no maid servant could marry without the consent of her parents, her master, the magistrate and minister. If they failed to comply with the law, the minister and servant were subject to severe censure and punishment by the courts. ...Few if any servants bothered to follow the established procedure, causing a great deal of distress in the colony. The problem became pressing by 1640 when the Assembly again undertook to keep servants from marrying without going through the proper channels. Any servant man who secretly married without the master's or mistress's consent should have one additional year added to the indenture time. The maid servant who married secretly received a more harsh penalty--- her indenture time was doubled and corporal punishment was inflicted. A freeman who married a servant had to pay a fine of five hundred pounds

[2] Carry Me Back, p. 78.
[3] Ibid., p. 83, 84.
[°] Ibid., p. 112.
[¶] Ibid., p. 113.

of tobacco to the parish where the marriage took place, and he still did not get his wife until her indenture time had expired."[2]

"Freemen often found maids of their choice, forged the necessary written consent, and married them. For this offense the freeman had to pay the wronged master 1,500 pounds of tobacco or a year's service. His wife still had to finish the original service period plus an additional year or more and suffer a whipping."[3]

As would be expected, illegitimacy was not uncommon.

"By 1683, there were twelve thousand servants in the colony. This was approximately one-sixth of the total population."[°] "Servant status had no permanent stigma attached to it. Many of the most notable people in the colony had been indentured servants at some time in their lives. Following their indenture they expected to assume their proper position in the community as free persons."[¶]

"Many of the indentured servants in colonial Virginia would be considered...as maladjusted individuals. The harsh and severe atmosphere of the frontier community only accentuated this condition. Some could not adjust themselves to servitude or its requirements and sought release by the one method they knew to be certain---suicide. The number of deaths among indentured servants became so high after the middle of the seventeenth century that it was necessary to establish boards of inquest. The duties of these boards were to examine all servants who died of unknown causes and to decide how death had occured. The most common methods of suicide were drowning and hanging, according to the records of the boards of inquest."[®]

"After 1650...slavery was an accepted institution despite the fact that there was no statutory recognition of it."[•] An Act of March 1661 stated "'Negroes are incapable of making satisfaction (for time lost in running away) by addition of time.'...because the Negro was regarded as a servant for life."[£]

"Although Africans were early introduced into Virginia, importations were extremely slow during the first seventy years. The muster of 1625 included only twenty-three, all of whom were on the Western shore."[*] In 1681 "the number of slaves was placed at three thousand. Not until that date was the population and further importation of slaves of any importance. The white servant still dominated the labor scene."[+] "From 1690 to 1700 a great increase in African headrights was discernible" and they "became the most important basis for the acquisition of land."[#]

"An early statute...passed on August 4, 1619, declared that all men owning servants must enter their names, terms of indenture, and conditions with the Secretary of State, under a penalty of forty shillings fine. In addition, any person bringing in servants followed the same procedure within one month of their arrival. This applied to Indian servants as well as to white servants and, later to Negro servants and slaves."[§]

[2] Carry Me Back, p. 113.
[3] Ibid., p. 114.
[°] Ibid., p. 75.
[¶] Ibid., p. 72.
[®] Ibid., p. 93.
[•] Ibid., p. 10.
[£] Ibid., p. 11.
[*] Ibid., p. 23.
[+] Ibid., p. 25.
[#] Ibid., p. 26.
[§] Ibid., p. 47.

"The Indian servant was on the same level with the white servant. Some laws were more stern in their application to Indians...since the colonists wished to avoid conflicts with the neighboring tribes. The Indian servant had the same rights, privileges, and duties as the white servants."[2] "At no time in Virginia's history, however, was there any great number of Indians held either in temporary or permanent bondage."[3]

"Because of the rather delicate relations existing between the white colonists and the adjacent tribes, an early Virginia law specified that no Indian servant could be owned except with the special license of the governor...but there was no uniformity of enforcement."[3]

"Slavery was prevalent among the Virginia Indian tribes, and was practicd by the colonists on some Indian captives taken in raids, despite its illegality."[°]

"Most...Indians therefore remained servants up to 1671." There had been "specific acts...passed in 1654, 1661, and 1670 prohibiting Indian slavery and guaranteeing to servant Indians all rights enjoyed by English servants," but "...by the acts of 1676, 1679, and 1682, slavery was applied to the Indian. At first it merely included those captured in war by the soldiers. But finally it was applied to all Indians sold by neighboring tribes to the colonists. Moreover, the Indian's property was regarded as free plunder, open to depredation by the soldiers."[¶]

"Many Indian parents were quite anxious that their children should be servants of the white colonists who would educate them in the fundamentals of learning and Christianity, and teach them English. ...Indian children placed with Virginians were to be treated as white servants, were not to be transferred to another under any pretense, and were to be free at the age of twenty-five years."[°]

"Indians servants were subject to the same taxes as other servants. Levies had to be paid for them by their masters. Indian women were charged with levies the same as Negro women."[®]

The older tax lists mention slaves by name and constitute one of the best sources for tracing black ancestry. By checking court order books, deeds, and wills of families who owned slaves and tracing their route of migration, you can often determine the parentage of the slaves since many generations of slaves would stay in the same family. When slaves were bought and sold at auction, it considerably complicates the situation.

THE MILITIA

"American military history began with the establishment of the Virginia colonial militia in the seventeenth century. Although ill-trained, it was the colony's only defense against Indian attacks and invasion by hostile powers."[•]

"On the frontier every man over the age of 16 was required to render military service" and "to answer the muster call six times each year."[£] The fine lists contain names of men who missed the muster call and were fined for their absence. Many of these men will also be listed in the delinquent tax rolls---along with the county or state they migrated to.

[2] Carry Me Back, p. 41.
[3] Ibid., p. 42.
[°] Ibid., p. 45.
[¶] Ibid., p. 46.
[®] Ibid., p. 48.
[•] Virginia's Colonial Soldiers by Lloyd D. Bockstruck
[£] The Militia Of Washington County, VA 1777-1835 by Gerald H. Clark

The military "size rolls" "...routinely give the soldier's place of birth, age, residence, occupation, and physical description. And sometimes this was made even more informative when the enlisting officer recorded his impression of the soldier."[2]

The militia's finest hour came on the 7th of October, 1780 at the Battle of King's Mountain---the turning point in the Revolutionary War.

Major Patrick Ferguson's threat "to the officers on the Western waters of Watauga, Nolachucky, and Holston, that 'if they did not desist from their opposition to the British arms, he would march his army over the mountains, hang their leaders, and lay their country waste with fire and sword.' ...accomplished more than Ferguson bargained for."[3] The militia commanders of the respective districts---Sevier, Shelby, and Campbell---decided to take action on their own and march over the mountains after Ferguson.

Leaving enough militia in their counties to protect the settlements from the Cherokees and Tories, the remaining militia gathered for the journey. The frontier militia of Sullivan Co. had 240 men commanded by Isaac Shelby, Washington Co. had 240 men commanded by John Sevier, and Washington Co., VA had 400 men commanded by William Campbell. They were joined by the militias of Wilkes and Surry Co. who had 350 men commanded by Benjamin Cleveland and smaller groups of militia and volunteers from NC, SC, and GA.

Ferguson, his Rangers, and Loyalist militia retreated and made their stand on what Ferguson considered an untakeable position---King's Mountain. The colonial militias made repeated attacks that were repulsed before the final assault. The battle lasted one hour and ended with the death of Ferguson and the total defeat of his British forces.

The action was not under state or continental control or command---it was fought by volunteers and militia without any authorization, so the men did not claim it in their pension records. If they had failed in their mission, the militia commanders would probably have been brought before Congress on charges.

In colonial times, "tax districts...paralleled the militia districts" and were "laid out originally to include the number of young males best suited to the operation of a military company. A district's tax receiver was the elected militia captain." The name of a district would change when a new captain was elected, "even though the bounds remained the same." Militia districts were later numbered, but "many tax rolls...continued to be" named "for the captain."[o]

The law was later changed and every male between 18 and 45, who was physically fit, and of good moral character in theory belonged to the militia. This does not appear to have included Indians or Negroes. "The 1820 census" has two "overlapping categories---one for males 16-26 and another for" males 16-18 "who were still under the age for obligatory military duty."[¶]

When the men "mustered" or trained, it was often a time when the prowess of the younger men was tested by bullies. The militia gradually became a paper army that never served. As the Civil War approached, it had already became a social club in some areas instead of a military organization---picnics were held at the musters. Often they did not

[2] Virginia's Colonial Soldiers by Lloyd D. Bockstruck
[3] King's Mountain And Its Heroes by Lyman C. Draper, p. 169.
[o] "Using "People Finders" To Track Individuals Not Cited Therein: The Example Of Georgia's Saunders Worthington" National Genealogical Soc. Quarterly, Vol. 83, No. 2, June 1995, p. 97.
[¶] Ibid., p. 99.

meet at all. Many states had already disbanded their militias before
the Dix Act was passed---which formed the National Guard and abolished
the state run militias.

The oath of allegiance is another valuable record that places
individuals in a particular place at a particular time. The Virginia
General Assembly directed the oath be taken during the Revolutionary
War. The figures in some of these lists evidently show the age of the
individual who took the oath.

A memorandum of the Inhabitants of Henry County of those that hath taken
the oath of allegiance. Sept. 13th, 1777.

Fred* Rives

Tully Choice Sr.	71	Jesse Hall	30
Tully Choice	24	Isham Hall	26
William Choice	21	Lanceford Hall	25

THE DAUGHTERS

Tax lists do not name the daughters because they were not tithable.
However, if you check marriage records, deeds, surveys, and court orders
during the period you are researching, you may be able to determine the
parentage of a female. The tax lists will list the male or males with
that surname who were tithable and this is often good circumstancial
evidence. If the lists are dated, the names of neighbors and relatives
may appear in the court records and this will be further verification.
Few of the early settlers left wills so it is often hard to determine
maiden names. This method is especially helpful for the period before
census records were kept.

Alphabetized or semi-alphabetized lists make it almost impossible to
determine who the next door neighbors were because the dates were
usually not included. This situation makes research in the surveys,
deeds, and court order books (especially the road orders) essential.
Families moved together and the son-in-law and daughter would often
immigrate with their parents, brothers, sisters, uncles, aunts, and
cousins.

ILLEGITIMACY

Illegitimacy and sexual promiscuity have always been detrimental to
the welfare of a society and to the children so most governments in the
past have tried to regulate the conduct of individuals for the common
good. Fines were imposed on females who had a baseborn child and/or the
father of the child---if it could be proven in court. In truth, there
were many instances where the mother never knew who the father actually
was.

The illegitimate male children will appear in the household of their
mother---if they had not been bound out and were still living at home---
when they become tithable. This establishes their birthdate and the
maternal side of the family, but whether or not the paternal side can be
established depends on court records and family tradition. The father
sometimes claimed the child or left some type of inheritance that was
recorded in the deed or will books. And a child would sometimes take
the surname of the illegitimate parent.

There is little hope of identifying the daughters unless there is some mention of them in the mother, father, or grandparent's deeds, wills, estate settlements, or the court orders. One possibility is that a brother or uncle may name a sister or neice in certain records or she may live with or near them.

BOUND OUT

A difficult and frustrating problem arises when your ancestor appears in a county without an individual of the same surname ever being mentioned in the records. The tax lists often will provide answers. If the surname does not appear in an adjoining county, the family may not have stayed in the area very long or they may have died and the child was bound out. There is also a possibility the child was illegitimate, bound out in another county or state and came to the present county with the family he was living with, adopted, or was orphaned and brought to the county by friend or relatives.

This would be a good time to discuss the census records. From 1790 to 1840, the censuses only listed the head of the household by name and ticked off the number of males, females, and slaves in each category. In this period, it is almost impossible to determine the number of children in a particular family. The common mistake is to assume all the children in the census record belonged to the family, but this was not the case---there were children bound out, grandchildren, orphans staying with families, hired laborers, relatives living with families, and older people placed in households by the court for their care and maintenance. The census records were taken June through September and at this time of year it was a common practice to keep children to help with the farm work and housework. And remember that the mortality rate was high and many families had numerous children who never reached adulthood.

In colonial times, some parents bound out their children as apprentices to learn a trade. An apprentice was also classified as a servant. The important difference "between the status of apprentice and that of servant or slave was that an apprentice could not be sold." Their duties were also different. "A servant could be put to any task within reason by his master. Articles of agreement signed by apprentice and employer usually included a provision that the apprentice would not work in the fields, that all his attention should be devoted to learning his trade." And "when an apprentice was forced to labor in the fields instead of at this trade, he lost valuable time. Time was money in the estimation of the courts, and the apprentice should be reimbursed."

"The term of apprenticeship was not established by law as was the term of the indentured servant."[2]

"The Assembly in 1647 provided that two children, whose parents could neither support nor educate them, should be sent to James City to work in the public flax houses." And "in 1672, the same body commanded the county courts to bind out all poor children to tradesmen, who would teach them a trade. At the end of their term, these, as well as all apprentices, were given corn, clothes, a cow and calf, and a rifle according to custom. Refusing to provide these allowances, the master was brought to court where sentence was passed."[3]

"Many Negro children received much the same opportunities for apprenticeship as did the white children. This applied principally to free Negroes, who were able to apprentice their children even after

---

[2] Carry Me Back, p. 66.
[3] Ibid., p. 67.

slavery had been sanctioned legally." And "the county courts protected the rights of the free Negro almost as zealously as those of the Whites."[2]

Floyd Co., KY Court Order Books

9 March 1874. "Ordered that John Irick a...poor child of this county 12 years of age be bound as an apprentice to L.D. Clark Sr. until he shall arrive at 21 years of age, to be taught the art, trade and business of a farmer. And also reading, writing, and common arithmetic including the rule of these. And to provide him with a good new suit of clothes at the termination of said apprenticeship and that the said apprentice shall have proper medical attention and shall be well fed and clothed and treated with humanity."
24 Nov. 1823. "Ordered that Susannah Nolin, aged about four years, be bound unto Isaac Fleetwood to be taught and instructed in the art and business of spinster and seamstress."
21 Dec. 1818. "Thadeus Remy is not to be bound out as it appears from evidence that John Remy, his grandfather, takes care of him."

Floyd Co., KY Circuit Court Book

July Term 1820. "Ordered that it be certified to the auditor of public accounts that the satisfactory proof was this day made in open court that Fanny Mautt an insane person of whom inquisition was had and taken at the July circuit court 1818 of this court still continues in about the same state of lunacy and insanity and that the allowance for her support and safekeeping is continued at $120 per year to be paid quarter yearly and Rhodes Meade is continued committee."

DATES OF ARRIVAL AND DEPARTURE

Tax lists can be used in conjunction with censuses and other records to determine accurate dates of arrival and departure. They are often the only records that show when an ancestor moved to another county.

1820 Scott Co., VA Census

Levi Conn   1 0 0 0 1 0   2 0 0 1 0

1820 Floyd Co., KY Census

Levi Conn   1 0 0 0 1 0   1 0 1 1 0

A comparison of the two census records shows that Levi Conn emigrated from Scott Co., VA to Floyd Co., KY sometime between the dates the censuses were taken, but when you add the tax lists you may be able to determine a more accurate date.

1820 Scott Co., VA Tax List

Levi Conn   1 - - 2   (No date)

Unfortunately, in this case, the above list was undated and the 1820 Floyd Co., KY Tax List is missing. If dates for both 1820 tax lists had available, the period of emigration could have been closely determined.

[2] Carry Me Back, p. 67.

Another valuable record in determining dates of arrival and departure is the county court order books which list exemptions, tax deliquents, and militia appointments.

Floyd Co., KY Court Order Books

Feb. 1809. "Stephen Adams exempted from payment of the levy of 1807, as he having proven that he paid the levy in the State of North Carolina."
"Mark Foster exonerated from the levy of 1808 and future levies."
May Term 1809. "Robert Meade enters motion that he be exempted from paying future levies on his man slave, Isaac, due to infirmity of indigestion. The motion overruled."
Oct. Term 1809. "On the motion of David Branham, Sr., ordered that his Negro man, Daniel, a slave, be exempted from future levies."
Feb. Term 1812. "Benjamin Ellis' Negro boy, listed as at 16, to be taxed in 1811."
27 Nov. 1815. "William Johnson enters his list of taxable property for 1815; to-wit: 1 tithe, 4 horses at $150.00 and 461 acres of 3rd rate land at 1 dollar. Total amount $581.00."
25 Nov. 1822. "Ancil Jarrell exempted from working on roads and paying county levy."

WAGON TRAINS

One of the more interesting aspects of tax lists is that they can be used for social and historical studies. They contain not only what individuals owned, but often other notes of interest. The land taxes sometimes list whether the land was 1st, 2nd, or 3rd rate and who made the orginal survey---which is essential in establishing the location of land. Perhaps, the most interesting aspect is that they can be used to compile the probable composition of wagon trains and migration to and from an area.

David Washington Austin's description of his family's migration states: "Our stay in North Carolina was only temporary. Two years after leaving Grayson (VA), we were ready to move on to newer country. So on November 15, 1855, father gathered together all his earthly possessions, including his wife and the ten children that had been born, and made ready. His family, another family, and a few others loaded all they had in five wagons pulled by two yokes of oxen and three teams of horses."

"The journey was slow and tedious. We covered about twenty miles a day, camping at night in any good place we could find. We were on the road a little more than a month, arriving in Wise, Virginia, December 20."

"There were twenty-nine in the company. There were twelve in our family, twelve in John Poplin's family, with Jim Ashly, Abe Gooch, Enoch Cox, Jesse Parsons, and Bets Howell completing the company. Besides the horses and oxen pulling the wagons, there were two other horses and five head of cattle---four milk cows and a heifer."[2]

A family would often stop for a year or two to raise crops before moving to another county or state. They may not have owned land or have been involved in any court proceedings so tax lists are often the only evidence they were ever in a county.

It was common for families, extended families, and neighbors to move together. Sometimes sons and daughters married along the way and families would stop along the route. There were also cases where a

[2] Pioneer Recollections, p. 15.

family would migrate to another state or county, decide to move back for some reason, and then return to the same area many years later.

MAPS AND MIGRATION

It is extremely important to know when a county was formed and the parent county or counties it was formed from when you are doing research. As new counties were formed, the boundaries changed and an ancestor will often still be living in the same place even though there may have been a number of counties formed from the original county over the intervening years. As an example; if an ancestor states they were born in Patrick Co., VA in 1760, they would actually have been born in the western section of Halifax Co.---which became Pittsylvania Co. in 1767, Henry Co. in 1776, and Patrick Co. in 1790. There is a list of formation dates of VA, NC, KY, and TN counties in the back of this book.

The reasons why a family migrated are varied, but usually it was in search of a better life. Always keep a map handy of the area you are researching. There were few migration routes so it is relatively simple to determine migration patterns for the area you are researching. An inexpensive, but useful book is U.S. Migration Patterns by Wendy L. Elliott---which includes maps and general information on migration patterns.

"In 1723, the Lords of Trade of London, upon the petition of the Virginia Council, exempted the inhabitants of Spotsylvania and Brunswick from the payment of quit rents and the purchase of land rights for the space of seven years" in order to encourage settlement on the frontier. "The French settlements to the west of the [Blue Ridge] mountains constitued a" threat "to the future development of the colony, and inducements were offered to settlers who would...make their homes in the two new counties."[2]

The western lands of Brunswick were only sparsely settled and in Nov. 1738 to encourage settlement on the Roanoke it was enacted "'Whereas the lands lying upon Roanoke River on the southern boundary of this colony are for the most part unseated and uncultivated; and a considerable number of persons, as well as his Majesty's natural born subjects, as foreign protestants, are willing to import themselves with their families and effects, and to settle upon the said lands, in case they can have suitable encouragement for their so doing: And whereas this settling of that part of the country will add to the strength and security of the colony in general...therefore, be it inacted that all persons whatsoever who within ten years next after the passing this Act shall import themselves into this colony, and settle upon the Roanoke River, on the south branch (Dan) of the same above the fork; and on the north branch of said river, above the mouth of Little Roanoke, and the lands lying between them, deemed to be in Brunswick County, shall be exempted from the payment of all levies for ten years, and be at liberty at all times hereafter to pay the officers fees in money at the rate of three farthing per pound of tobacco.'"

"'And that letters of naturalization be granted to any alien settling there.'" The only requirement was "'that the persons so settling upon the lands before mentioned shall during the said ten years support their own poor and make and maintain their own bridges without any charge upon the rest of the parish of St. Andrews and County of Brunswick.'"

"The "Aliens" to whom the government was offering the above inducements to settle in old Brunswick were the Germans, the Quakers,

[2] The History of Pittsylvania County Virginia, p. 33.

and the Scotch-Irish who were then moving in great numbers from Pennsylvania down into Virginia."[2]

"Parishes were laid out co-extensive with the counties, which were later divided and sub-divided as settlement increased. The administration of the...parish was in control...of the vestry." They arranged and provided "for religious worship of the people of the parish" and safe guarded "the morals of the community, it was also incumbent upon the vestry to care for the poor, collect taxes and mark the boundary lines of land."[3]

The Great Wagon Road began near Philadelphia and ran westward in Pennsylvania to the Blue Ridge, crossed this range, and thence southwestward from Pennsylvania across Maryland, and down the Shenandoah Valley of Virginia between the Blue Ridge and Alleghaney Mountains, crossed the Blue Ridge at the Staunton River water gap and passed through the present counties of Bedford, Franklin, and Henry, entered North Carolina, and ended at the Yadkin River. Another fork led to Fort Chiswell on the New River, to a point of junction with the Richmond Road, which ran from Richmond, Virginia, to Fort Chiswell.

About the time of the aforementioned act, "'Lord Granville's agents were disposing of desirable lands in the Piedmont region of North Carolina to settlers at the rate of three shillings proclamation money for six hundred and forty acres...and was making large free grants on the condition of seating a certain portion of settlers.'"[o]

In 1755, after Braddock's defeat in the French And Indian War, the fear of Indian attacks spread across the frontier and "'hundreds of families'" deserted "'the exposed lands adjacent to the upper waters of the Potomac, James, and Staunton Rivers,'" and "'thousands poured out of the foothills of Piedmont'" Virginia and fled to the Carolinas. In a letter, the Reverend James Maury of Louisa County described the "condition in Piedmont Virginia: 'By Bedford Courthouse in one week 'tis said, and I believe truly said, near 300 persons, Inhabitants of this Colony, past, on their way to Carolina...Scarce do I know a neighborhood but what has lost some families, and expects to quickly lose more.'"[¶]

The Proclamation of 1763 stated no one was to take up lands "beyond the heads or sources of any of the rivers which fall into the Atlantic Ocean" and that anyone settled on such lands "should remove themselves from such settlements." Few individuals who had already settled on this land complied with the decree. In 1767, the land west of the Blue Ridge was opened up for settlement by a treaty with the Indians.

The unfair taxation and injustice of Governor Tryon in NC led to the Revolution of the Regulators---which ended with the Battle of Alamance on May 16, 1771. Many of the early settlers fled westward to the Watauga Settlements to escape punishment.

In the late 1760s and early 1770s, a group of hardy pioneers settled along the Watauga River, on the Long Island of the Holston River, at the forks of the Holston, and along the Nolichucky River---these were the Over the Mountain Men who would later turn the tide of the Revolutionary War at King's Mountain.

In 1772 the settlers "formed the Watauga Association after leasing land that is now in Tennessee from the Cherokee Indians. North Carolina had ordered the settlers to leave because the state claimed the land,

[2] The History of Pittsylvania County Virginia, p. 37.
[3] The History of Pittsylvania County Virginia, p. 114.
[o] Sunlight On The Southside, p. 22.
[¶] The History of Pittsylvania County Virginia, p. 65, 66.

but they refused." According to <u>An Adventure In Northeast Tennessee</u> by Faith Stahl, "The Wataugans bought the land after the Transylvania Purchase, but asked North Carolina's protection from the British and Indians. The men of the settlement signed a petition to be annexed by North Carolina in July 1776. By 1777, the North Carolina Assembly formed the Washington District into a county...and later forced land-holders to pay a fee, allowing them to keep only 640 acres they had previously purchased."

"In 1784, representatives from several militia companies met in Jonesborough and formed a bill of rights for a new, seperate state from North Carolina." "John Sevier was elected chairman of the state, then called Frankland, and Anglo-Saxon word meaning "land of the free," and was made governor in 1785." The name was later changed to Franklin.

"North Carolina had given the land to the federal government to pay its share of the war debt in 1783, leaving the settlers with no government, it rescinded the cession the next year and proceeded with efforts to reclaim the land."

"In early 1788...Sevier and his followers met on the battlefield with a group of North Carolina loyalists led by John Tipton" and "it's said to be the only battle Sevier ever lost."

"During the four years Franklin did exist, settlers in the area were subjected to a double dose of governmental control---taxes, marriage licenses, deeds, county courts, militias,"[2] etc.

"Due to constant danger from marauding Indians, all of the settlers became "Indian Fighters." They had to have a certain proficiency to survive, and the fact is that most did not. Of the 256 who signed the papers forming the Watauga Association in 1772, scarcely a dozen were living ten years later. Of these, only one had died a natural death."[3]

"In the spring of 1779," Isaac Shelby was "elected a member of the Virginia Legislature from Washington County; and, in the fall, he was commissioned a Major by Governor Jefferson for the escort of guards to the Commissioners for extending the boundary line between Virginia and North Carolina. His residence was now found to be within the limits of the latter state, and he was, in November of this year, appointed by Governor Caswell a Colonel and magistrate of the new County of Sullivan, entering upon their duties at the organization of the County in February following."[o] In fact, both of Washington County's members of the General Assembly were living in the section that was North Carolina. The other member was William Cocke.

The boundary change caused some problems for the tax collector--- which were recorded in the following court order:

20 Oct. 1779 Washington Co., VA. "On complaint of the sheriff against William Cock for Insulting and obstructing Alexander Donaldson Deputy Sheriff when collecting the publick Tax about the Thirtieth of September last and being Examined saith that being at a point on the North side of Holston River in Carters Valley collecting the publick Tax the said William Cock as he came to the Door of the House in which said sheriff was doing business said that there was the sheriff of Virginia collecting the Tax and asked him what right he had to collect Taxes there as it was in Carolina and never was in Virginia and he said the people was fools if they did pay him publick dues and that he dare him

[2] "The Lost State Of Franklin" Appalachian Quarterly, Vol. 1, No. 2, Sept. 1996, p. 4, 5.
[3] "The Nolichucky Settlements An Overview" by George E. Jackson Jr. Appalachian Quarterly, Vol. 1, No. 2, Sept. 1996, p. 52.
[o] King's Mountain And Its Heroes by Lyman C. Draper, p. 412, 413.

to serve any process whatever that he said Cock undertook for the people upon which sundry people refused to pay their Tax and some that had paid wanted their money back again."
"Ordered that the conduct of William Cock respecting his obstructing and insulting and threatening the sheriff in Execution of his office be represented to the Executive of Virginia."
"Ordered that if William Cock be found in this county that he be taken into custody and caused to appear before the Justice at next court to answer for his conduct for obstructing the Sheriff in Execution of his office."

The land north of the Holston River was thought to be in Virginia prior to the survey. Finally, the state of Tennessee was formed in 1796.
"In 1779-80 the Virginia-North Carolina dividing line was extended westward to the firt crossing of the Cumberland River. From this point west to the Mississippi, Thomas Walker surveyed the line for Virginia, following generally the established eastern course of 36°30'. The Walker survey was by no means a thorough or efficient one. Most of the boundary had to be located through dense virgin forests and much of it over rugged mountainous terrain. The rest followed stream courses, where it was equally difficult to establish precise boundaries."
"Westward from the top of the Cumberland Mountain, the boundary between Virginia" (after 1792, Kentucky) "and North Carolina (after 1796, Tennessee) remained in doubt from the Walker survey in 1779 until 1859...when the Cox-Peebles survey party blazed a 320-mile path across the same terrain...from New Madrid Bend to Cumberland Gap. They marked this boundary permanently, they hoped, by erecting three-foot high stone slabs every five miles, beginning at Compromise on the Mississippi River and placing the final stone just below the point where the old Wilderness Road passed through the Cumberland Gap."
"The Kentucky Bend, or New Madrid Bend, carved in the" Mississippi River "by the earthquake of 1811, created a geographical quirk, leaving a portion of Kentucky's Fulton County an "island" accessible only by ferry or, by land, via Tennessee."
"The Kentucky-Missouri boundary is 'a line drawn through the center of the Mississippi River.'"[2]
When the "Walker Line" was in effect "TN came over the KY line on the average of 20 miles all along what is the current state line." And "if your ancestor came from east TN, chances are they may have been included on censuses for KY/TN/NC because this a very mountainous region. The settlers actually never knew which state and county they really lived in. Many Sullivan Co., TN early records may even be found in Lee Co., VA! The census taker" or tax collector "never knew where he was in those mountains. If a TN resident on the 1820 TN census was born before 1796, then technically, he was born in NC!"
"This is absolutely the worst area of the United States to research because of all of the above. Unfortunately, you can't be sure you've checked all resources until you've checked KY/TN/NC"[3] and South West VA.
Land near the Virginia-North Carolina border in Wilkes Co., NC (later Ashe Co.) was thought to be in Montgomery Co., VA (later Grayson Co.)---so it is necessary to check the records of neighboring Virginia counties if your ancestor lived near the North Carolina border. There were similar boundary disputes and mistakes between counties within Virginia and North Carolina.

[2] The Kentucky Encyclopedia, p. 102, 103.
[3] Southern Bailey's With Branches Upwards & Outwards, Vol. 1, No. 1, p. 18.

"The border between North and South Carolina had long been in dispute and it wasn't until 1772 that the matter was settled. Prior to this North Carolina had issued more than 1,000 grants for land in an area that is now South Carolina---in what are the present counties of Marlboro, Chesterfield, Lancaster, York, Chester, Union, Cherokee, Spartanburg, Greenville, Laurens, and Newberry, an area which was then thought to be in the North Carolina counties of Bladen, Anson, Mecklenburg, and Tryon."[2]

An ancestor was sometimes charged with taxes in two counties or states. And sometimes they were missed by the census taker or tax collector.

"In September, 1773, Daniel Boone, with his own and five other families, set out from the Yadkin Valley, North Carolina, to settle in Kentucky. A company of forty other men joined the party on the way. They drove their hogs and cattle before them, and carried their baggage and provisions on pack-horses. When near the Cumberland Gap they were suddenly attacked by Indians and six of the party were killed, among these was Boone's son." "The Boones and other...members of the party desired to push on, but finally, were persuaded to return; some went to their own homes, and others to those of friends on the Clinch River."[3]

The first permanent settlement in Kentucky occured "as early as June, 1774," when "Captain James Harrod and thirty companions began a settlement at Harrodstown, and still other settlements were started at Boiling Springs and St. Asaph's, better known as Logan's Station."[°]

"The Transylvania Company...settled territory that was a part of Virginia, and...they had no claim to it except that based upon the purchase they had made from the Cherokees...at Sycamore Shoals"[¶]---on "March 17, 1775, giving...the Transylvania Company all the lands lying along and between the Ohio, Kentucky, and Cumberland Rivers. This vast tract of fertile land comprised most of the present state of Kentucky and a part of Tennessee."[®] "Governor Dunmore of Virginia issued a proclamation denouncing 'one Richard Henderson and other disorderly persons' because they had 'set up claim to lands of the crown within the limits of the colony.' This action...caused the settlers to resist the right of the Transylvania Company to sell the land, and to deny its power to make a good title to it."[¶]

"Henderson and Company...requested 'that Transylvania be added to the number of the United Colonies,' and" expressed "the earnest wish that the 'Proprietors of Transylvania be considered by the Colonies as broters engaged in the same great cause of liberty.' This message was...referred to the Virginia delegation because the territory in question was a part of Virginia's domain. Patrick Henry and Thomas Jefferson both opposed the action of Congress...on the ground that Kentucky was a part of Virginia, and, therefore, not under the control of the Continental Congress. In the meantime, eighty-four settlers who had entered land in the office of the Transylvania Company had drawn up another petition" that they "be taken under the protection of the Colony of Virginia, that the titles of their lands might be made secure, and that they might be protected from the taxes imposed by the Transylvania Company."[•]

"On December 7, 1776, the Virginia Assembly passed an act asserting the right of the state to all her western claims, known as Fincastle

[2] North Carolina Land Grants In South Carolina
[3] Kentucky The Pioneer State Of The West, p. 35.
[°] Ibid., p. 41.
[¶] Ibid., p. 46.
[®] Ibid., p. 43.
[•] Ibid., p. 49, 50.

County, and divided this vast territory into three sections---Kentucky, Montgomery, and Washington Counties. This act...established the government of the Kentucky settlements under the rule of Virginia."[2] "In 1780 Kentucky County, Virginia was divided into three Kentucky counties---Fayette, Lincoln, and Jefferson."[3] And "On February 4, 1791, an act to admit the state into the Union June 1, 1792, was passed by Congress and signed by President Washington."[o]

There were two main roads to Kentucky---"pioneers were compelled to pass north around the spurs of the Alleghaney Mountains and float down the Ohio River, or travel overland through the Cumberland Gap, at the southeastern extremity of the State."[¶]

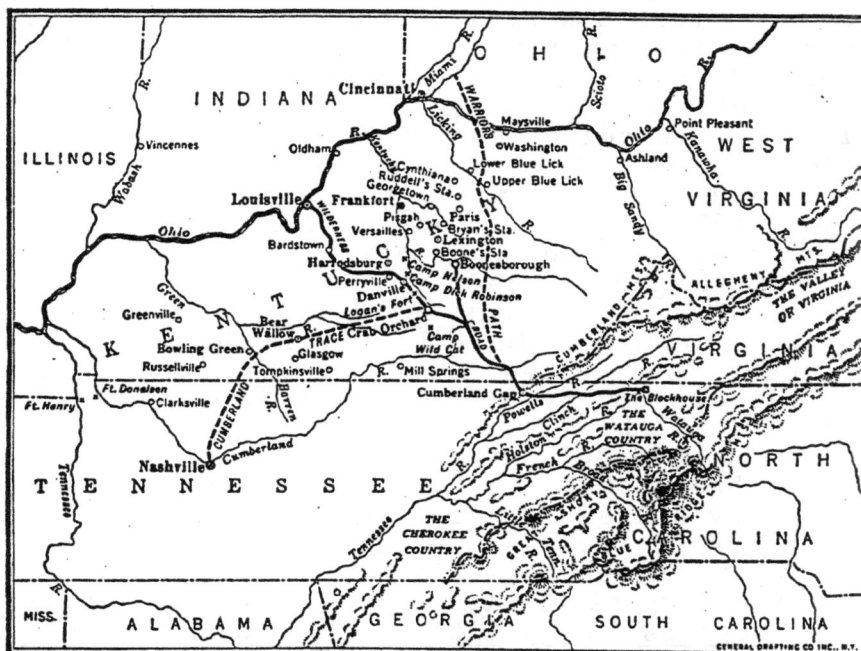

MAP OF PIONEER ROADS

"From a fort called "The Blockhouse," located on the Watauga River in North Carolina, to Boonesborough, the Wilderness Road passed over about two hundred miles of rugged forest-covered hills and mountains. The "trail," as marked by Boone, led from the Watauga River in East Tennessee to Moccasin Gap near Gate City, and extended along the old trail to Powell's Valley, and passed down this to the Cumberland Gap. Thence Boone followed the "Warrior's Path" across a ford of the Cumberland just below Pineville Gap, thence down the Cumberland to Flat Lick. Here he took the old Buffalo Trail which led to Hazel Patch, near Rockcastle River, thence up around Stone Creek to Boone's Gap, two miles southeast of Berea, and on to Otter Creek and Kentucky River, where he built Boonesborough."[®]

Many researchers simply do not realize the enormous amount of territory encompassed by some of the early Virginia and North Carolina

[2] Kentucky The Pioneer State Of The West, p. 51.
[3] Early Kentucky Settlers. The Records of Jefferson County, Kentucky from the Filson Club History Quarterly.
[o] Kentucky The Pioneer State Of The West, p. 121.
[¶] Ibid., p. 59.

counties. For example; "In 1745, when Augusta County, Virginia was erected, its domain extended from the Alleghenies to the Mississippi River, and from the northern part of Tennessee to the Great Lakes."[2] And "twenty-four counties in North Carolina and all of Tennessee have been formed from the area that once constituted Rowan County,"[3] North Carolina.

I would highly recommend Virginia Counties: Those Resulting From Virginia Legislation by Morgan P. Robinson. This book "accurately shows the dates of formation of Virginia counties, the territory from which they were formed, their boundaries and jurisdiction, and the origin of their names---and backs up the information with documentation. While only 100 Virginia counties exist today, at least 172 were created at one time or another by Virginia legislation. Numerous counties became extinct, merged with other counties or changed their name, while others were cut off to form the states of Kentucky and West Virginia."

Two books helpful in tracing the arrival and migration of ancestors are Cavaliers And Pioneers, Abstracts of Virginia Land Patents and Grants 1623 - 1732 (three volumes) by Nell M. Nugent and Northern Neck, Virginia, Land Grants 1694 - 1862 (four volumes) by Gertrude E. Gray. A useful companion book to Nugent's Cavaliers And Pioneers is Early Virginia Immigrants 1623 - 1666 by George C. Greer. "This is a list of immigrants to Virginia...who were not original patentees of land." The Complete Book Of Emigrants series by Peter W. Coldham may also be helpful. Another useful book is Map Guide To The U.S. Federal Censuses, 1790 - 1920 by William Thorndale and William Dollarhide. "This work shows all U.S. county boundaries from 1790 to 1920. On each of the nearly 400 maps the old county lines are superimposed over the modern ones to highlight the boundary changes at ten-year intervals."

If your ancestor stopped in the Caribbean before migrating to America, there are three books that might be helpful: Bermuda Settlers Of The 17th Century by Julia E. Mercer which contains "abstracts of the earliest known records of Bermuda Settlers...many of the early settlers of Bermuda---or their descendants---removed to the mainland and were among the pioneer settlers of the Carolinas, Georgia, and Virginia;" The Original Lists of Persons of Quality...and Others Who Went From Great Britain to the American Plantations, 1600 - 1700 by John Camden Hotten; and Omitted Chapters From Hotten's Original Lists of Persons of Quality. While working in the Public Record Office in London, Hotten recognized the importance of the 1679/80 Barbados Census---the most comprehensive census of any English colony in the seventeenth century. "Thousands of immigrants settled on Barbados before planting new roots on the mainland...parish registers give the names of all of those baptized or buried, with the dates and the names of the family members; the census returns list landowners' names with the number of freemen, servants, and slaves in the household; and the militia rolls list the militiamen by regiment and company, as well as the landowners responsible for furnishing troops."

REPLACEMENT OF RECORDS LOST OR DESTROYED

One of the first things you learn when you begin researching your family is that many of the early records have been lost or destroyed--- especially the ones you often need the most! Tax lists can be used to construct fairly accurate "censuses" of the area you are researching.

[2] Chronicles Of The Scotch-Irish Settlement In Virginia, Extracted From The Original Court Records Of Augusta County, 1745 - 1800 by Lyman Chalkey.

[3] A History Of Rowan County, North Carolina by Rev. Jethro Rumple.

The land tax records indicate who owned land in a county even if the deed books have been lost or destroyed. If the tax lists are dated or the name of the nearest neighbor is listed, they can be used to determine the approximate location of the land. Personal Property Tax Lists are often the most helpful because they list what an ancestor owned that was taxable and sometimes contain other valuable information.

A nickname---or the location of their dwelling in a county---is often used to differentiate betwen two people with the same name. As an example; David Gentry ("Long David") or John Carter ("Big Head"), John Adums ("at Pigg River") and John Addums ("In Ye Forrest"). Also, they will often be referred to as Sr., Jr., the "elder", or "son of".

The 1790 census schedules for the areas that constituted the present states of Deleware, Georgia, Kentucky, New Jersey, Tennessee, and Virginia; the entire 1800 census; and portions of the 1810 census (18 counties in Virginia) were destroyed when the British burned Washington during the War of 1812. The Reconstructed 1790 Census of Georgia Substitutes for Georgia's Lost 1790 Census by Marie De Lamar and Elisabeth Rothstein, the "First Census" of Kentucky 1790 by Charles B. Heinemann, 1800 "Second Census" of Kentucky by G. Glenn Clift, the 1770 - 1790 Census of the Cumberland Settlements: Davidson, Sumner and Tennessee Counties by Richard C. Fulcher, The 1787 Virginia Census (which contains the tax lists for the entire state of Virginia and Kentucky County) by Nettie Schreiner Yantis, Early Virginia Tax Payers 1782 - 87 Other Than Those Published by the United States Census Bureau by Augusta B. Fothergill and John Mark Naugle, and A Supplement to The 1810 Virginia Census by Nettie Schreiner Yantis use tax lists and other records as replacements for the missing census schedules.

On Jan. 10, 1921, an accidental fire destroyed most of the 1890 Census. "It was estimated that 50 percent of the census schedules were damaged by water and 25 percent destroyed by the actual fire. The records were laid out to dry but were never rebound. On Feb. 21, 1933, Congress authorized the destruction of what was left of the original population schedules."[2] However, a few scattered fragments of the 1890 Census survive for ten states and the District of Columbia.

The 1890 Census can be reconstructed by using the 1890 tax list (which contains 100 categories); the 1890 Special Schedules of Surviving Soldiers, Sailors, and Marines and Widows (which also sometimes list the names of Confederate veterans or their widows---the names are often crossed out); school censuses; the surviving deeds, wills, court orders, marriage bonds and licenses; survey books; etc.

The 1890 tax list gives an indepth inventory of almost every conceivable type of taxable property---and the categories for Males over 21, Legal Voters, Nearest Resident (for those who owned land), Enrolled Militia, and Children between 6 and 20 years old make this tax list an invaluable asset when reconstructing the 1890 Census. By comparing the 1890 tax list with the 1880 and 1900 Censuses and the 1880 to 1890 tax lists, it is possible to determine many of the children in the between 6 and 20 category and children who were already in their own households when the 1890 Census was taken. The number and ages of children also allow you to match a family with previous records and seperate two individuals with the same name---even if neither owned land.

The Agricultural Schedules, Industrial Schedules, Mortality Schedules, Slave Schedules, and Social Statistics are often neglected by researchers, but they are important records---and they can also be used to reconstruct "censuses."

[2] 1890 Census Data Loss A "Research Disaster" by Thomas S. Watson, Associated Press.

BRIDGING THE GAP AND BETWEEN WHEN COUNTIES WERE FORMED

Tax lists allow researchers to bridge the gap between censuses. If your ancestor was born between the ten-year interval of the census records, you can use tax lists to determine his age and sometimes his parentage. Counties were formed during this ten-year interval and the first tax list of the new county is also the first "census". By comparing the tax list or lists of the county or counties from which the new county was formed, you can determine the county your ancestor lived in and the approximate area where he lived prior to the formation of the county. There were many individuals who migrated into a county for a short time and left without ever buying or surveying land or being mentioned in the court records---tax lists are often the only evidence they were ever there.

Many males would have reached a tithable age and many females would have married before the next census was taken. And some males would have died leaving no other records to indicate they had ever existed--- having never married, owning no property, and leaving no heirs.

Remember! Tracing the daughters can be a problem. A simple way to find out who they married is to notice the families who lived near them and were mentioned in deeds and court orders with them. When they removed to another county or state, the son-in-law and daughter would often move to the same area and reside near the father or a brother on or near the same creek where they lived. There is no sure-fire method for tracking the daughters, but this is the least complicated method to use when consent papers, deeds, or wills are not available and provides a starting point for further research.

1837 FLOYD CO., KY TAX LIST

WHAT THEY DON'T SHOW IS IMPORTANT

One important thing to remember is what tax lists don't show is also important. They can either be used to prove or disprove genealogical, historical, or social information.

The ancestry of Booker Mullins Sr. is a good example of how to check tax records. He migrated to Floyd Co., KY ca 1810 (the surviving tax lists begin in 1837) and appears in the 1810 census along with Ambrose Mullins Sr., Ambrose Mullins Jr., William Mullins, John "Buttin John" Mullins, Solomon Mullins, and Joshua Mullins. Ambrose Sr. and John were the sons of William Mullins Sr. (see page 10) and Joshua was the son of John Mullins of Charlotte Co., VA---Ambrose Jr. and William appear to be the sons of Ambrose Sr. and Solomon was the son of John. Two sons of William Mullins Jr.---another son of William Mullins Sr.---later appear in Floyd Co., KY as does John Mullins the brother of Joshua Mullins. The mystery is who was the father of Booker Mullins?

According to the undocumented work of other researchers, Booker Mullins was b. 1762 - d. 1865 (at 102 years old); married Polly Bench, Nancy Stanley, or Judith Stanley; and was the son of William Mullins Jr. and his wife Jane Stanley. The question is how accurate is this information?

An indepth examination of the early Virginia and North Carolina tax records reveal that Booker Mullins first appears in the 1788 Montgomery Co., VA Tax List and that the name Booker is only associated with the William Mullins Sr. line. And the name was passed down through the descendants of William Mullins Jr.---his son Booker married Judith Stanley on 12 May 1803 Franklin Co., VA. Ambrose Mullins (Sr.) also appears in the 1788 tax list.

1788 Montgomery Co., VA Tax List C

Booker Mullins	1	0	0	Aug. 26	(no tithe)
Moses Standley	0	0	0		
Nehemiah Prater	0	0	3		
Ambrose Mullins	0	0	2	Aug. 30	
Nenian Prater	0	0	0		

Always notice the tithable age and the column headings in the tax lists you are checking. Column number one is white males above 16 and under 21, column number two is slaves, and column number three is horses.

In 1789, Booker appears in the tax list, but Ambrose Mullins is in the Franklin Co., VA tax lists. Nehemiah Prater and Nenian Prater are also missing from the 1789 Montgomery Co., VA Tax List.

1789 Montgomery Co., VA Tax List C

Booker Mullins	0	0	0	Aug. 19	(Burks Fork and Greasy Creek, Indian Ridge)
Moses Standley	0	0	0	---- --	(No date given)

From Survey Book D, page 269; Thomas Patteson---4275 acres at head waters of Laurel Fork in Burks Fork of Big Reed Island adjacent to Huff. Chainmen: Newman (Nenian?) Prater & William Mullan. Pilots: John Edins & Moses Standley. 17 Nov. 1790.[2]

In 1787, Ambrose Mullins was in list A and Moses Standley, Nehemiah

[2] Montgomery County, Virginia - Circa 1790, p. 54, by Netti Schreiner Yantis.

Prater, Ning (Nenian?) Prater, and John Eedens were in list B of Henry Co., VA. William Mullans was in list B of Franklin Co., VA.

List of those persons who were fined in 1787 for not attending muster--- and who did not appear in the tax lists [they having apparently moved].[2]

Soldier: John Mullins   Captain: Jones

Captain Jones' militia company was part of James Newell's district (List A) which bordered North Carolina. Byrd Smith's district (List C) bordered Henry Co., VA.

The 1788 tax list indicates that Booker Mullins probably married in late 1787 or early 1788---between the two tax lists---and that he appeared in his own household prior to being taxable in 1789. Notice the male 16 to 21 had disappeared from his household in 1789 and Booker had became tithable. The 1789 tax list allows us to estimate Booker's birth date as ca 1768.

The Booker Mullins who married Judith Stanley first appears in the 1801 Franklin Co., VA Tax List and his will was probated 1 April 1867 Franklin Co., VA. From the available records, there is strong circumstancial evidence that Booker Mullins Sr. was the son of William Mullins Sr. and the brother of Ambrose Sr., John "Buttin John", and William Mullins Jr.

MARRIAGE DATES

An approximate marriage date can be obtained by noting the year a male appears as head of his own household, but there will be exceptions. Another less reliable method is to note the year the first male became tithable in a household and count backwards---this method should only be used when there are no prior records for an ancestor and their county or state of origin is unknown. The problems with this method are numerous ---there may have been daughters born before the first male, there may have been other males who became tithable and were already in their own households before your ancestor appeared in the area, there may have been illegitimate children, there may have been a prior marriage, etc.-- but, you can establish an approximate marriage date and birth date for your ancestor.

TAX LISTS AND TRADITIONS

Tax lists are helpful in proving and disproving family traditions. The reliability of any tradition depends upon the individuals who passed it from generation to generation, the accuracy of the retelling (some individuals and families tended to exaggerate and add details), and how accurately the generation and lines the tradition pertains to has been preserved. There will be minor discrepancies in any family tradition no matter how accurate the tradition is.

As an example; according to Bob Elkins, an older member of our Elkins line, family tradition states our Elkins "came from Sword's Creek, VA." Sword's Creek is located in NE Russell Co., VA near the Tazewell Co., VA border. The marriage record of Charles Elkins, the son of James Elkins who first appears in the 1840 Pike Co., KY Census, states he was born in Tazewell Co., VA. Checking the 1830 Russell Co., VA Census, I found a James Elkins with a wife and children who match the exact age brackets of the James Elkins household in the 1840 Pike Co., KY Census.

[2] Montgomery County, Virginia - Circa 1790, p. 28, by Netti Schreiner Yantis.

1840 Pike Co., KY Census

James Elkins	1 1 1 0 0 1	1 1 2 1 0 1

1830 Russell Co., VA Census

James Elkins	1 0 0 0 1	2 1 0 0 1 0 0 1
Thomas Elkins	0 0 0 0 1	2 0 0 1
Joseph Booth	1 0 0 1 1 0 1	0 0 0 0 1
John Booth	0 0 0 0 1	2 0 0 0 1

In 1820, James Elkins does not appear in Russell Co., VA, but an Elijah Elkins is listed in the census index. Deeds indicate Elijah Elkins lived on Indian Creek which is located in SE Russell County near the Tazewell Co., VA border.

Index to 1820 Virginia Census - Russell County

Elijah Elkins	138A	Stephen Booth	133A
Absalom Elkins	138A	William Booth	133A
Joseph Elkins	138A	Joseph Booth	133A
William Elkins	138A		

In 1830, Elijah Elkins; his sons John and Joseph; and William Booth were in Lee Co., VA. Elijah's wife Jerusha (Booth) Elkins d. Aug. 1856 on Powell's River in Wise Co., VA---Wise Co. was formed in 1856 from portions of Lee, Scott, and Russell Co., VA.

1810 Russell Co., VA Tax List - Wilson Vermillion's List

Elijah Elkins	2 0 3	March 23
Michael Sword	1 0 4	
Stephen Booth	2 0 2	March 22
Henry Sword	1 0 1	March 21

The parentage of Elijah Elkins is also unknown, but Richard Elkins Sr. is listed with a tithable male above 16 and under 21 in his household in the 1789 Montgomery Co., VA Tax List. Elijah Elkins married Jerusha Booth, d/o Stephen and Nancy Booth, on 28 Nov. 1789 in Montgomery Co., VA.

1788 Montgomery Co., VA Tax List

Richard Elkins Sr.	0 0 1	April 30	List B
Richard Elkins Jr.	0 0 3		
Drury Elkins	0 0 3		
James Elkins	0 0 1		
Zachariah Elkins	1 0 1	(no tithe)	
Archibald Elkins	0 0 6	Oct. 18	List C
Stephen Booth	0 0 2	Dec. 19	

1789 Montgomery Co., VA Tax List

Richard Elkins Sr.	1 0 1	Feb. 20	List B
Richard Elkins Jr.	0 0 2	(Walkers and Wolf Creeks, Clear	
Drury Elkins	0 0 3	Fork of Wolf Creek)	
Zachariah Elkins	0 0 2		
Archibald Elkins	0 0 5	March 6	List C

	(Falling Spring, Burks Run, Dry Branch of Little River)		
Stephen Booth	0 0 0	March 8	
	(Both sides of Little River; Dry Branch, Sugar Run, South Fork and West Fork of Little River; Meadow and Mill Creeks, Dunkard Bottom or Mahanaim)		

1782 Tax Lists of Virginia

Archibald Elkins	1	0	Montgomery County
James Elkins	1	0	Henry County
Nathaniel Elkins	1	0	Henry County
Robert Elkins	1	0	Washington County
Ralp Elkins	1	0	Montgomery County

First Land Surveys In Washington County, Virginia

1783 April 25	Richard Elkins	200 acres	Clinch River	
1782 April 25	Richard Elkins	179 acres	Upper North Fork Clinch River	
1781 Aug. 29	Richard Elkins	400 acres	Clinch (actual Settlement in 1773)	

1772 Botetourt Co., VA Tax List

Nathaniel Elkins	1	Jessey Elkins Senr.	1
Ralf Elkins	1	Ralf Elkins Junr.	1
Jesey Elkins	1	Richard Elkins	1

1767 Pittsylvania Co., VA Tax List
List of Tithes taken by Peter Perkins for the year 1767

Ralph Elkins Jr.	
Richard Elkins	1 tithe
Nathaniel Elkins	son Jessey
James Elkins	on Leatherwood
Jesse Elkins	1 tithe

Halifax Co., VA - "In 1753 Thomas Calloway and others were ordered to view improvements made on Leatherwood Creek (Henry County) by Ralph Elkins, and found 26 acres under cultivation, 20 head of neat cattle, fences, orchards, buildings, and other improvements to the values of £396."[2]

1749 Lunenburg Co., VA Tax List

Ralph Elkins, Ralph Elkins Jr.	2
Richard Elkins	1

1750 Lunenburg Co., VA Tax List

Ralph Elkins, Ralph Elkins Jr.	2
Richard Elkins	1

Richard Elkins Sr. would have been born ca 1727/28 or earlier (based on his probably being 21 or over in the 1749 tax list).

[2] History of Pittsylvania County Virginia, p. 60.

Now back to the Russell County, Virginia tax records for information on James Elkins and his probable father Elijah Elkins. Column number one is tithables, column number two is horses.

1797 - 1832 Russell Co., VA Tax Lists

Year	Name	Tith.	Horses		Year	Name	Tith.	Horses	Date
1797	Elijah Elkins	1	1		1823	Elijah Elkins	3	3	
1798	Elijah	1	1			James	1	1	
1799	Elijah	1	1			John	1	1	
1800	Elijah	1	1			Jospeh	1	2	
1801	Elijah	1	1			William	1	0	
1802	Elijah	1	1		1824	Elijah	3	4	
1803	Elijah	1	1			James	1	1	
1804	Elijah	1	1			John	1	1	
1805	Elijah	1	1			Joseph	1	2	
1806	Elijah	1	1			William	1	0	
1807	Elijah	1	0		1825	Elijah	–	3	
1808	No Record					James	–	1	
1809	Elijah	1	2			John	–	1	
1810	Elijah	2	3			Thomas	–	1	
1811	Elijah	2	3			William	–	1	
1812	Elijah	2	4		1826	Elijah	1	2	
	Absalom	1	0			James	1	1	
1813	Elijah	3	4			John	1	0	
1814	Elijah	3	4			Joseph	1	2	
	Absalom	1	1			Larkin	1	0	
1815	Elijah	3	4			Stephen	1	1	
	Absalom	1	1			Thomas	1	1	
1816	Elijah	4	4			William	1	1	
	William	1	1			Absalom	1	0	
1817	Elijah	2	2		1827	Elijah	2	3	March 7
	Joseph	1	2			James	1	1	March 25
	William	1	1			John	1	1	March 24
	Absalom	1	0			Joseph	1	1	
1818	Elijah					Stephen	1	2	
	Joseph	1	2			Thomas	1	1	March 15
	William	1	1			Absalom	1	0	May 10
	Absalom	1	1		1828	Elijah	2	3	
1819	Elijah	3	2			James	1	1	
	Joseph	1	2			John	1	2	
	William	1	1			Joseph	1	1	
	Absalom	1	1			Stephen	1	2	
1820	Elijah	3	0			Thomas	1	1	
	Joseph	1	3			Absalom	1	0	
	William	1	1		1829	Elijah	2	3	Feb. 4
	Absalom	1	1			James	1	1	March 9
1821	Elijah	2	–			John	1	2	
	John	1	–			Joseph	1	1	
	Joseph	2	–			Thomas	1	1	Feb. 4
	William	1	–			Absalom	1	0	March 9
	Absalom	1	–		1830	James	1	1	
1822	Elijah	2	2			Thomas	1	1	
	James	1	1		1831	James	1	1	March 2
	Joseph	1	1			Thomas	1	0	
	William	1	0		1832	James	1	1	
						Stephen	1	1	
						Thomas	1	1	

James Elkins appears in his own household in the 1822 tax list which indicates he was born ca 1805/06 or earlier and probably married in late 1821 or early 1822. There were no Elkins listed in Tazewell Co., VA in 1820. According to the 1850 Pike Co., KY Census, James' oldest daughter Cynthia was born ca 1824 in Virginia (1822 would probably be a more accurate date).

In the Tazewell Co., VA court orders, Zachariah and Absalom Elkins are mentioned in 1806. Zachariah Elkins and Rachel his wife of Kanawha Co., VA made a deed to Frederick Cooke of Wolf Creek, Tazewell Co., VA in 1807. In 1810, Zachariah, Richard (Jr.), Daniel, and James Elkins were in Cabell Co., VA.

In the Lee Co., VA court orders, Joseph Elkins, William Elkins, John Elkins, Thomas Elkins, Elijah Elkins, and Larkin Elkins were listed as road hands on 21 Sept. 1846.

Richard Elkins Sr., Richard Elkins Jr., William Elkins, and Zachariah Elkins were listed in the 1800 Wythe Co., Va Tax List. Tazewell County was formed in 1799 from Russell and Wythe County. The 1796, 1798, and 1799 Russell and Wythe County petitions to form Tazewell Co., VA were signed by Richard Elkins Sr., Richard Elkins Jr., William Elkins, Daniel Elkins, and R. Elkins. Richard Elkins Sr., Richard Elkins Jr., Drury Elkins, and Zachariah Elkins were in list B of Wythe Co., VA in 1793. Wythe was formed in 1789 from Montgomery and Grayson County. Montgomery Co., VA was formed in 1776-77 from Fincastle County.

James Elkins is listed in the 1790 Personal Property Tax Lists of Russell Co., VA---he later moved to Clark Co., KY. In the 1788 land tax records; Drury Elkins 200 acres, James Elkins 400 acres, Richard Elkins 400 acres. In 1787, Drury Elkins and Jesse Elkins are in the Russell Co., VA tax lists; Richard Elkins and Archibald Elkins are in the Montgomery Co., VA tax lists. Russell County was formed in 1785 from Washington County. The Petition of Dec. 9, 1785 for the Division of Washington County, Virginia was signed by Drury Elkins, James Elkins, and Jesse Elkins. Washington Co., VA was formed in 1776-77 from Fincastle County.

After crossing the Blue Ridge [Mountains], Richard, Ralf, Nathaniel, Jesey, Ralf Jr., and Jessey Elkins Jr. were in Botetourt Co., VA in 1772 ---Fincastle Co., VA was formed from Botetourt County in 1772. By 1753, Ralph Elkins Sr. was living on Leatherwood Creek (present Henry County) in Halifax Co., VA. Halifax County was formed in 1752 from Lunenburg County. In 1767, Ralph Jr., Richard, Nathaniel, Jesse, and James Elkins were in Pittsylvania Co., VA. Pittsylvania County was formed in 1766-67 from Halifax County. Henry Co., VA was formed in 1776-77 from Pittsylvania County. In 1749 and 1750, Ralph Elkins Sr. was living in the section of Lunenburg County that became Charlotte Co., VA.

I have used the available records in this section to show how a proper knowledge of the tax records, migration patterns and routes, and county formation can be used to establish a probable ancestry for an ancestor. All conclusions should be carefully researched and documented by additional records, but this is a helpful method for starting your research. The 1832 - 1840 Russell Co., VA and Pike Co., KY tax lists should show when James disappeared from one list and appeared in the other.

An overview of the preceding records seem to indicate James Elkins was the son of Elijah & Jerusha (Booth) Elkins; Elijah was the son of Richard Elkins Sr.; and Richard Sr. was the son of Ralph Elkins Sr.--- who was born ca 1700-05. Richard Elkins Sr. was the father of Richard Jr., James, Drury, Zachariah, and Elijah Elkins. Richard Jr. married Nancy (Leslie) McGuire 2 Dec. 1787 Montgomery Co., VA and James married Molly Jackson 23 Sept. 1782 Washington Co., VA. Ralph Elkins Sr. was the father of Richard Sr., Ralph Jr., Nathaniel, Jesey Sr., and James Elkins.

A comparison list of the children of James Elkins can be created by using the 1830 Russell Co., VA Census; the 1840 and 1850 Pike Co., KY Censuses; and Floyd and Pike Co., KY marriage records.

The 1840 Pike Co., KY Census will be used as the connection between the 1830 Russell Co., VA and the 1850 Pike Co., KY Censuses.

1840 Pike Co., KY Census

```
James Elkins          1 1 1 0 0 1      1 1 2 1 0 1
                      @ ® °       +     = •  3 2   -
                                           *
```

+ James Elkins b. 1803 VA [head of household # 781 in 1850 Pike Co.]

- Elizabeth b. 1785? VA [wife of James, household # 781 in 1850 Pike Co.] The 1850 Census is hard to read and the birth date may be inaccurate---the 1830 and 1840 censuses place her birth date between 1800 and 1810.

2 Cynthia b. 1824 VA [household # 691 in 1850 Pike Co.] married Samuel Robinson/Robertson 4 Nov. 1841 Pike Co., KY.

3 Rebecca b. 19 Aug. 1824 VA [household # 748 in 1850 Pike Co.] married John Davis 18 Feb. 1845 Pike Co., KY.

° William Fletcher b. 1828 VA [household # 774 in 1850 Pike Co.] married Elizabeth Lyons 23 Nov. 1848 Pike Co., KY.

* Emmeriah (America) b. 1830 VA [household # 39 in 1850 Floyd Co.] married Rhodes W. Meade 21 Jan. 1849 Pike Co., KY. Emmeriah and Rhodes are living with his parents, Moses & Polly (Hackworth) Meade.

• Rhoda Jane b. 1832 VA [household # 781 in 1850 Pike Co.] married John Hale on 20 March 1854 Pike Co., KY. Her tombstone states b. 11 Nov. 1830 - d. 5 Jan. 1913.

® John H. b. 1834 VA [household # 781 in 1850 Pike Co.] married Sarilda Shortridge 8 Nov. 1860 Pike Co., KY.

= Alice Ann (Allisa/Alcy) b. 1835 VA [household # 781 in 1850 Pike Co.] married James H. "Pharmer" Leslie.

@ Charles A. b. 1837 VA [household # 781 in 1850 Pike Co.] married Lorena Stratton 7 Feb. 1861 Floyd Co., KY.

There were four additional children in the James Elkins household in 1850:

Louisa A. b. 1840 VA married Daniel J. Harrison 21 July 1858 Pike Co., KY. Louisa is listed as born in Virginia, but the 1840 Pike Co., KY Census would seem to indicate she was probably born in KY.
James H. b. 1843 KY married Julia Ann Walker 10 Dec. 1865 Pike Co., KY.
Lorenzo D. b. 1844 KY
Samuel Jefferson b. 1847 KY married Marinda Maynard 20 Aug. 1872 Pike Co., KY.

The above birth dates were based on the ages listed in the 1850 Pike Co., KY Census. There can be a year variation in the birth dates--- depending on the month an individual was born. And there is always the possibility an individual's age was turned in wrong or the census taker made a mistake.

James Elkins and his wife, Elizabeth (Priest?), had one more child before she died ca 1851:

Mary Elizabeth b. 11 Nov. 1850 Pike Co., KY - d. ca 1903 Floyd Co., KY married Samuel Clark 15 Aug. 1872 Pike Co., KY.

BUILDING FAMILY UNITS

The goal of all genealogical research is to build family units. As previously shown, when tax records are used properly---and in conjunction with other records---it is much easier to document family relationships. The tax lists are an effective and efficent means of proving ancestry by themselves, but when used with other records the possibilities are greatly expanded. Tax lists allow you to use the whole family approach to research and like census records they allow you to have an overview of the area you are researching.

WHERE TO FIND TAX RECORDS?

One of the major problems in any field of research is finding the records you need. The same is true with tax records. Few of these records remain in county courthouses----many have been lost or destroyed. The state archives have most of the surviving original copies of the tax records, but microfilmed copies can be ordered from the archives, private companies, or through an LDS Family History Center. There have been a few helpful books published on the early Virginia and North Carolina tax lists: Virginia Tax Records From The Virginia Magazine of History And Biography, The William and Mary College Quarterly, and Tyler's Quarterly; North Carolina Taxpayers 1701 - 1786 and North Carolina Taxpayers 1679 - 1790 by Clarence E. Ratliff.

CHAPTER THREE: COUNTY FORMATION

A knowledge of the formation date and parent county/counties that encompassed the area you are researching is essential. It is both time saving and vital to good research. The following chapter contains all pre-1800 Virginia, North Carolina, Kentucky, and Tennessee counties; and counties of special interest to researchers in southwestern VA, northeastern NC, eastern KY, and eastern TN.

VIRGINIA

County	Formation Date	Parent County/Counties
Accomack	1634	Northampton
Albemarle	1744	Goochland, Louisa
Amelia	1734	Brunswick, Prince George
Amherst	1758	Albemarle
Augusta	1738-45	Orange
Bath	1790-91	Augusta, Botetourt, Greenbrier
Bedford	1753	Albemarle, Lunenburg
Botetourt	1769	Augusta
Brunswick	1720	Prince George, Isle of Wight, Surry
Buchanan	1858	Russell, Tazewell
Buckingham	1758	Albemarle
Cabell		
Campbell	1781-82	Bedford
Caroline	1727-28	Essex, King and Queen, King William
Charles City	1634	Original Shire
Charlotte	1764-65	Lunenburg
Chesterfield	1749	Henrico
Culpepper	1748	Orange
Cumberland	1748-49	Goochland
Dickenson	1880	Buchanan, Russell, Wise
Dinwiddie	1752	Prince George
Elizabeth City	1634	Original Shire
Essex	1692	Old Rappahannock
Fairfax	1742	Prince William
Fauquier	1758	Prince William
Fincastle	1772	Botetourt (discontinued 1777)
Fluvanna	1777	Albemarle
Franklin	1785	Bedford, Henry
Frederick	1738-43	Orange
Giles	1806	Montgomery, Monroe, Tazewell
Gloucester	1651	York
Goochland	1727	Henrico
Grayson	1792-93	Wythe
Greenbrier		
Greensville	1780	Brunswick, Sussex
Halifax	1752	Lunenburg
Hanover	1720	New Kent
Henrico	1634	Original Shire
Henry	1776-77	Pittsylvania
Illinois	1778	Augusta (discontinued 1784)
Isle of Wight	1634	Original Shire
James City	1634	Original Shire

Kanawha		
Kentucky	1777	Fincastle (discontinued 1780)
King and Queen	1691	New Kent
King George	1720-21	Richmond, Westmoreland
King William	1701-02	King and Queen
Lancaster	1651	Northumberland, York
Lee	1792-93	Russell
Loudoun	1757	Fairfax
Louisa	1742	Hanover
Lower Norfolk	1637	New Norfolk
Lunenburg	1746	Brunswick
Madison	1792-93	Culpepper
Mathews	1790-91	Gloucester
Mecklenburg	1764-65	Lunenburg
Middlesex	1673	Lancaster
Montgomery	1776-77	Fincastle
Monroe		
Nansemond	1637	Upper Norfolk
New Kent	1654	York
New Norfolk	1636	Elizabeth City
Norfolk	1636	Lower Norfolk
Northampton	1634	Original Shire (prior to 1642 was called Accawmack)
Northumberland	1648	Indian District of Chickacoan
Nottoway	1788-89	Amelia
Orange	1734	Spotsylvania
Patrick	1790-91	Henry
Pittsylvania	1766-67	Halifax
Powhatan	1777	Cumberland, Chesterfield
Prince Edward	1753-54	Amelia
Prince George	1702-03	Charles City
Prince William	1730-31	King George, Stafford
Princess Anne	1691	Lower Norfolk
Old Rappahannock		(abolished 1692)
Richmond	1692	Old Rappahannock
Rockbridge	1778	Augusta, Botetourt
Rockingham	1778	Augusta
Russell	1785	Washington
Scott	1814	Lee, Russell, Washington
Shenandoah	1772	Frederick (Dunmore until 1778)
Smyth	1832	Washington, Wythe
Southampton	1749	Isle of Wight, Nansemond
Spotsylvania	1720-21	Essex, King and Queen, King William
Stafford	1664	Westmoreland
Surry	1652	James City
Sussex	1753-54	Surry
Tazewell	1799	Russell, Wythe
Upper Norfolk	1637	New Norfolk
Warrosquoyacke	1634	(Changed to Isle of Wight in 1637)
Warwick	1634	Original Shire
Washington	1776-77	Fincastle
Westmoreland	1653	Northumberland
Wise	1856	Lee, Russell, Scott
Wythe	1789	Montgomery
Yohogania	1776	Augusta (discontinued 1786)
York	1634	Original Shire (changed from Charles River)

NORTH CAROLINA

Albemarle	1663	1 of 3 original counties (discontinued in 1739)
Anson	1749	Bladen
Ashe	1799	Wilkes
Archdale	1705	(Changed to Beaufort in 1712)
Bath	1696	(discontinued in 1739)
Beaufort	1705	Bath
Bertie	1722	Chowan
Bladen	1734	New Hanover
Brunswick	1764	New Hanover
Buncombe	1791	Burke, Rutherford
Burke	1777	Rowan
Bute	1764	(discontinued in 1779)
Cabarrus	1792	Mecklenburg
Camden	1777	Pasquotank
Carteret	1722	Bath
Caswell	1777	Orange
Chatham	1770	Orange
Chowan	1670	Prec. Albemarle
Craven	1705	Prec. Bath
Cumberland	1754	Bladen
Currituck	1671	Albemarle
Dobbs	1758	Johnston (discontinued in 1791)
Duplin	1749	New Hanover
Edgecombe	1741	Bertie
Franklin	1778	Bute
Gates	1778	Chowan, Hertford
Glasgow	1791	(discontinued 1799)
Granville	1746	Edgecombe, Original Glasgow
Greene	1799	Dobbs or Glasgow
Guilford	1770	Rowan, Orange
Halifax	1754	Edgecombe
Hertford	1754	Bertie, Chowan, Northampton
Hyde	1705	Wickham Prec. Bath
Iredell	1788	Rowan
Johnston	1746	Craven
Jones	1778	Craven
Lenoir	1791	Dobbs
Lincoln	1778	Tryon
Martin	1774	Halifax, Tyrrell
Mecklenburg	1762	Anson
Montgomery	1778	Anson
Moore	1784	Cumberland
Nash	1777	Edgecombe
New Hanover	1729	Craven
Northampton	1741	Bertie
Onslow	1734	(Preceding Bath)
Orange	1752	Bladen, Granville, Johnston
Pasquotank	1671	Prec. Albemarle
Perquimans	1671	Prec. Albemarle
Person	1791	Caswell
Pitt	1760	Beaufort
Randolph	1778	Guilford
Richmond	1779	Anson
Robeson	1786	Bladen
Rockingham	1785	Guilford
Rowan	1753	Anson

Rutherford	1779	Burke, Tryon
Sampson	1784	Duplin, New Hanover
Stokes	1789	Surry
Surry	1770	Rowan
Tryon	1768	(discontinued 1779)
Tyrrell	1729	Bertie, Chowan, Currituck, Pasquotank
Wake	1770	Cumberland, Johnston, Orange
Warren	1779	Bute
Washington	1799	Tyrrell
Watauga	1849	Ashe, Caldwell, Wilkes, Yancy
Wayne	1779	Craven, Dobbs
Wilkes	1777	Burke, Surry

KENTUCKY

Adair	1801	Green
Barren	1798	Green, Warren
Bath	1811	Montgomery
Boone	1798	Campbell
Bourbon	1785	Fayette
Boyd	1860	Carter, Greenup, Lawrence
Bracken	1796	Campbell, Mason
Breathitt	1839	Clay, Estill, Perry
Bullitt	1796	Jefferson, Nelson
Butler	1810	Logan, Ohio
Caldwell	1809	Livingston
Campbell	1794	Harrison, Mason, Scott
Carter	1838	Greenup, Lawrence
Casey	1806	Lincoln
Christian	1796	Logan
Clark	1792	Bourbon, Fayette
Clay	1807	Floyd, Knox, Madison
Cumberland	1798	Green
Elliott	1869	Carter, Lawrence, Morgan
Estill	1808	Clark, Madison
Fayette	1780	Kentucky County, Virginia
Fleming	1798	Mason
Floyd	1799	Fleming, Mason, Montgomery
Franklin	1794	Mercer, Shelby, Woodford
Gallatin	1798	Franklin, Shelby
Garrard	1796	Lincoln, Madison, Mercer
Grayson	1810	Hardin, Ohio
Green	1792	Lincoln, Nelson
Greenup	1803	Mason
Hardin	1792	Nelson
Harlan	1819	Knox
Harrison	1793	Bourbon, Scott
Henderson	1798	Christian
Henry	1798	Shelby
Hopkins	1806	Henderson
Jefferson	1780	Kentucky County, Virginia
Jessamine	1798	Fayette
Johnson	1843	Floyd, Lawrence, Morgan
Knott	1884	Breathitt, Floyd, Letcher, Perry
Knox	1799	Lincoln
Lawrence	1821	Floyd, Greenup
Letcher	1842	Harlan, Perry
Lewis	1806	Mason

Lincoln	1780	Kentucky County, Virginia
Livingston	1798	Christian
Logan	1792	Lincoln
Madison	1785	Lincoln
Magoffin	1860	Floyd, Johnson, Morgan
Mason	1788	Bourbon
Menifee	1869	Bath, Montgomery, Morgan, Powell, Wolfe
Mercer	1785	Lincoln
Montgomery	1796	Clark
Morgan	1822	Bath, Floyd
Muhlenberg	1798	Christian, Logan
Nelson	1784	Jefferson
Nicholas	1799	Bourbon, Mason
Ohio	1798	Hardin
Pendleton	1798	Bracken, Campbell
Perry	1820	Clay, Floyd
Pike	1821	Floyd
Pulaski	1798	Green, Lincoln
Rockcastle	1810	Knox, Lincoln, Madison, Pulaski
Scott	1792	Woodford
Shelby	1792	Jefferson
Warren	1796	Logan
Washington	1792	Nelson
Wayne	1800	Cumberland, Pulaski
Wolfe	1860	Breathitt, Morgan, Owsley, Powell
Woodford	1788	Fayette

TENNESSEE

Anderson	1801	Knox
Bedford	1807-08	Rutherford
Bledsoe	1807	Roane
Blount	1795	Knox
Campbell	1806	Anderson, Claiborne
Carter	1796	Washington
Claiborne	1801	Grainger, Hawkins
Cocke	1797	Jefferson
Davidson	1783	Washington
Dickson	1803	Montgomery, Robertson
Fentress	1823	Morgan, Overton
Franklin	1807	Bedford, Warren
Giles	1809	Maury
Grainger	1796	Hawkins, Knox
Greene	1783	Washington
Hamilton	1819	Rhea
Hancock	1844	Claiborne, Hawkins
Hardin	1819	Western District
Hawkins	1786	Sullivan
Hickman	1807	Dickson
Humphreys	1809	Stewart, Smith
Jackson	1801	Smith
Jefferson	1792	Greene, Hawkins
Johnson	1836	Carter
Knox	1792	Greene, Hawkins
Lincoln	1809	Bedford
Marion	1817	Indian Lands
Maury	1807	Williamson

McMinn	1819	Indian Lands
Meigs	1836	Hamilton, McMinn, Rhea
Monroe	1819	Roane
Montgomery	1796	Tennessee
Morgan	1817	Roane
Overton	1806	Jackson
Perry	1818	Hickman
Rhea	1807	Roane
Roane	1801	Knox
Robertson	1796	Tennessee
Rutherford	1803	Davidson
Sevier	1794	Jefferson
Shelby	1819	Hardin
Smith	1799	Sumner
Stewart	1803	Montgomery
Sullivan	1779	Washington
Sumner	1786	Davidson
Tennessee	1788	(County surrendered name when state became Tennessee in 1796)
Warren	1807	White
Washington	1777	(Covered present state of Tennessee and parts of the present state of North Carolina.)
Wayne	1785	(Abolished 1788. This Wayne County created under state of Franklin. Included present Carter County and part of Johnson County.)
Wayne	1817	Hickman
White	1806	Jackson
Williamson	1799	Davidson
Wilson	1799	Sumner

SAMPLE 1890 TAX LIST

FLOYD COUNTY, KENTUCKY

PRECINCT 5, PART NO. 26

STATE OF KENTUCKY

FLOYD COUNTY

TAX LIST

1890

THE NAME OF TAXPAYER, WHETHER RESIDENT OR NON-RESIDENT.	Land, each tract in acres	NEAREST RESIDENT.	Election Precinct in which situated.	Assessed value of each tract with its improvements.	City or Town Lots.	City or Town in which situated.	Assessed value of each lot with its improvements.	Number of Thoroughbred Stallions.	Value of Thoroughbred Stallions.
			1	2	4	5	6	8	9
Miller Samuel			5						
Moore Arthur			5						
Murphy John	50	Thomas Salesbury	5	50					
Neel Granville			5						
Malone Thomas			5						
Malone James			5						
Milliard Henry			5						
Milliard Nitro J.			5						
Mitchell Larkin			5						
McKinney Thomas	100	Jefferson Norvell	5	250					
" "	200	E. L. Storgell	5	400					
Neel Samuel	200	Judah Huton	5	500					
McKinley George	75	Mary Hager	5	100					
Morell T. H. B.	25	J. C. Ferguson	5	700					
"	25	T. M. Payne	5	50					
Osborn E. L.	100	David Runyons	5	300					
Perry David			5						
Perry Abraham			5						
Parson William	100	Isaac Parsons	5	200					
"	75	" " "	5	200					
Parson Isaac	100	William Parsons	5	100					
			5						
Perry James			5						
			5						
Ansell John W.	300	Elizabeth Rice	5	3000		Nonresident			
	45	John Akers	5	70					
			5						
Ratcliff Riley Heirs	50	Wm Storgell	5	500					
			5						
	100	E. L. Osborn	5	500					
	100	Henson Hamilton	5	350					
			5						
			5						
	80	Robin Clark	5	600					
			5						
			5						
			5	7870					

Number of Thoroughbred Geldings.	Value.	No. of Thoroughbred Mares and Colts.	Value.	No. of Stallions of common or mixed stock.	Value.	No. of Geldings, Mares, and Colts, of common or mixed stock.	Value.	No. of Mules and Male Colts.	Value.	No. of Jacks.	Value.	No. of Jennets.	Value.	No. of Thoroughbred Bulls.	Value.	No. of Thoroughbred Cows and Calves.	Value.	No. of Bulls, Steers, Cows and Calves of common or mixed stock.	Value.	No. of Sheep.	Value.	No. of Hogs over 6 months old.	Number Line.
20	21	12	13	14	15	16	17	18	19	20	21	22	23	24	25	26	27	28	29	30	31	32	
						1	60											2				6	1
						1	60											6	40	5	5	5	2
																		1		1	1		3
						1	50											4				1	4
																		1					5
																							6
																							7
																		5		6	6		8
						2	120											3				10	9
																		3					10
																							11
																		5	25	8	8	1	12
																		5		20	20	7	13
						1	60, 1	40										4					14
																							15
						2	100											8	10	20	20	9	16
																							17
																							18
																		1					19
																		1					20
						1	50											8	15	4	4	3	21
																							22
							75											7	15			1	23
																		2	20				24
						1	60											2					25
																		5		8	8		26
																							27
																		4		4	4		28
																							29
																							30
																							31
																							32
																						2	33
						3	200											3				3	34
						1	60											4					35
						1	40											1				1	36
																		1					37
						1	60											6	35				38
						1	75											5	15	2	2	6	39
																		2		6	6		40
						19	1070, 1	40										96	231	66	66	56	

Number Lines	Value	No. of Stores	Value	Value of Watches and Clocks	Value of Gold, Silver and Plated Ware	Value of Jewelry	No. of Diamonds	Value	Value of Household Furniture in excess of $300 worth	No. of Paintings other than Family Likenesses and Prints	Value	Value of Professional Library in excess of $200 worth	Value of Piano Fortes and other Musical Instruments	Value of Sewing and Knitting Machines over $30 in value	Value of Safes	Value of Wagons, Carriages, Barouches, Buggies, and vehicles of every description	Value of Raw Material to be used in Manufacturing	Value of Manufactured Articles
	33	34	35	36	37	38	39	40	41	42	43	44	45	46	47	48	49 21	50
1	18																	
2	10																	
3	2																	
4	4																	
5																		
6																		
7																		
8	5																	
9	50																	
10																		
11																		
12	4																	
13	15																	
14				15														
15																		
16	18																	
17																		
18																		
19																		
20																		
21	10																	
22																		
23	21																	
24																		
25																		
26				5														
27																		
28																		
29																		
30																		
31																		
32																		
33	8																	
34	10			5														
35																		
36	3																	
	12			5														
	14			50														

Value of Raw Material to be used in Manufacturing.		Value of Manufactured Articles.	Value of Manufacturing Implements and Machinery of all kinds.	Value of Agricultural Implements and Machinery in excess of $200.	Value of Agricultural Products of all kinds. (not raised this year.)	Value of Corporate Franchise.	Value of Slaughtered Animals.	Present Annual Value of Annuities and Royalties.	No. of Steamboats, Sailboats, or other Water Craft, or any interest therein.	Value.	Value of Patent Rights and value of Territory in which to sell patents.	Value of Steam Engines, including Boilers.	Value of Mineral Products, Oil, Gas and Salt Wells.	Value of all Wines, Whiskey, Brandies and substances thereof, not in Bond.	Miscellany—Value of all Property not hereinbefore specified.	Number Line.
49	49½	50	51	52	53	54	55	56	57	58	59	60	61	62	63	
																1
																2
																3
																4
																5
																6
																7
																8
																9
																10
																11
			10													12
																13
																14
																15
																16
																17
																18
																19
																20
																21
																22
																23
																24
																25
																26
																27
																28
																29
																30
																31
																32
																33
																34
																35
																36
																37
																38
																39
			15													40

	Number Name	Total Value of Real and Personal Property subject to Equalization.	Total Equalized Value of Real and Personal Property.	Credits or money at Interest either in or out of this State.	All other demands against Corporation in or out of this State.	Money in possession, or on deposit with Corporation or Persons in or out of this State.	Bonds of all kinds except U. S. Government Bonds.	Stocks not paid on by Corporation.	Value of all Judgments or Notes in suit or in the hands of another.	Value of all other property after deducting debts.	Total assessed value of Personal Property not subject to Equalization.	Grand Total value of Real and Personal Property upon which tax is to be collected.
		64	65	66	67	68	69	70	71	72	73	74
James	1	98										
Reuben	2	121										
John	3	53										
Greenville	4	54										
States	5											
Jane	6											
Sherman	7											
Nettie	8	6										
Clark	9	120										
	10	650										
	11											
Samuel	12	607										
George	13	117										
H. Bob	14	865										
	15											
E. C.	16	448										
	17											
	18											
David	19											
Elbridge	20											
Milton	21	482										
	22											
Isaac	23	197			50							50
Franc	24	20										
James	25	60										
James	26	13										
Arthur	27	3000										
Orpha	28	74										
Mary	29											
	30											
	31											
Wiley	32	500										
Arthur	33	8										
Harris	34	715										
Martin	35	410										
William	36	43										
Ben	37	695										
Bell	38	106										
		6										
		1498			50							50

Listed for Taxation in _Floyd_ County, Ky., for the Year 1880

Males over 21 years.	Legal Voters.	Enrolled Militia.	Children between 6 and 20 years.	No. of Bulls, Studs and Jacks.	Rates per season.	Tavern Licenses.	Pounds of Tobacco.	Pounds of Hemp.	Tons of Hay.	Bushels of Corn.	Bushels of Wheat.	Bushels of Oats.	Bushels of Barley.	Number Line.
76	77	78	79	80	81	82	83	84	85	86	87	88	89	
1	1	1	1							1110		50		1
1	1	1								400		10		2
1	1	1								150				3
										75				4
1	1	1	1							40				5
														6
1	1	1								100				7
														8
1	1	1	2							1100		100		9
			5							50				10
														11
1	1	1	2				50			500		50		12
										500				13
1	1	1	4							500				14
														15
1	1	1	4				10		2	250		20		16
														17
														18
1	1	1								40				19
1	1	1								300				20
1	1	1	4							500				21
														22
1	1		2							500				23
1	1	1												24
1	1	1								100		10		25
1	1		3						2	150				26
														27
			4							100				28
1	1	1					20							29
														30
														31
														32
1	1	1	4							50		10		33
1	1	1								250		110		34
1	1	1	3							250		30		35
										150				36
1	1	1								100				37
1	1	1	4							400				38
1	1	1	1						2	100		100		39
														40
28	28	25	141				80		6	5755		420		

Fifth Precinct, ... County ... Personal Property. Listed ...

Number Lines	Bushels of Clover and Grass Seed	Tons of Coal	Tons of Pig Metal	Tons of Bloom	Tons of Bar Iron	Number of Acres of Wheat		Number of Acres of Corn	Number of Acres of Meadow	Number of Acres of Woodland	Number of Cattle Exempt from Taxation	Value
	20	21	22	23	24	25		26	27	28	29	30
11								25			2	4
12								10			3	50
13								11		40 1		25
14								10				
15								4			1	15
16												
17								11				
18											3	30
19								30			3	20
10								9		60	5	30
11												
12								15			2	50
13								9		60	3	45
14								15		30	4	50
15												
16								11		10	6	50
17												
18												
19								21			1	20
20								10			1	20
21								26		100	6	50
22												
23								16		60	5	50
24											1	50
25								5			2	25
26								10			5	50
27										130		
28								5		55	4	35
29												
30												
31												
32												
33								5			1	15
34								10		250	4	40
35								8		10	2	40
36								8				
37								5			1	15
38								18		4	3	50
39								8	1		4	50
								768	1	1149	71	934

Summary of Part No. 26

Column No.	Acres or Lots.		
#1	1860	Land.	
#4		Town Lots.	

Column No.	KIND OF PROPERTY.	NUMBER.	Assessed Value.
8	Thoroughbred Stallions,		
10	Thoroughbred Geldings,		
12	Thoroughbred Mares and Colts,		
14	Stallions, common or mixed,		
16	Geldings, Mares and Colts, common or mixed,	19	1070
18	Mules and Mule Colts,	1	110
20	Jacks,		
22	Jennets,		
24	Thoroughbred Bulls,		
26	Thoroughbred Cows and Calves,		
28	Bulls, Steers, &c., common or mixed,	46	331
30	Sheep,	66	66
32	Hogs over six months old,	56	175
34	Stores,		
36	Watches and Clocks,		30
37	Gold, Silver and Plated Ware,		
38	Jewelry,		
39	Diamonds,		
41	Household Furniture over $350,		
43	Paintings, other than Family Likenesses, &c.,		
44	Professional Library over $350,		
45	Pianos, &c.,		
46	Sewing and Knitting Machines over $30,		
47	Safes,		
48	Wagons, Carriages, &c.,		
49	Raw Materials,		
	Amount carried up		1610

Column No.	KIND OF PROPERTY.	NUMBER.	Assessed Value.
	Amount brought up		1610
50	Manufactured Articles,		
51	Manufacturing Implements and Machinery,		
52	Agricultural Impl'ts and Mch'ry over $350,		
53	Agricultural Products,		18
54	Corporate Franchises,		
55	Slaughtered Animals,		
56	Annuities and Royalties,		
57	Steamboats, &c.,		
59	Patent Rights and Territory,		
60	Steam Engines and Boilers,		
61	Mineral Products,		
62	Wines, Whiskies, &c.,		
63	Miscellany,		
64	TOTAL		1628
66	Credits or Money at Interest, &c.,		
67	All other demands, &c.,		
68	Money in Possession,		50
69	Bonds of all kinds, except U. S.,		
70	Stocks not paid on by Corporations,		
71	Value of all Judgments, &c.,		
72	Value of all other Prop. after deducting debts,		
73	TOTAL		50
	Total Assessed Value of Personal Property,		
	TOTAL Subject to Taxation,		

General Statistics.

Column No.	ITEMS.	Number or Amount.	Column No.	ITEMS.	Number or Amount.	Column No.	ITEMS.	Number or Amount.
76	Males over 21 years,	25	85	Tons of Hay,	6	93	Tons of Bloom,	
77	Legal Voters,	25	86	Bushels of Corn,	5755	94	" Bar Iron,	
78	Enrolled Militia,	25	87	" Wheat,		95	Acres of Wheat,	
79	Children between 6 and 20 years,	80	88	" Oats,	420	96	" Corn,	
80	No. of Bulls, Studs and Jacks,		89	" Barley,		97	" Meadow,	
81	Rates per Season,		90	" Clover and Grass Seed,		98	" Woodland,	
82	Tavern Licenses,		91	Tons Coal,		99	Cattle exempt from Taxation,	
83	Pounds of Tobacco,	80	92	" Pig Metal,		100	Value of Cattle exempt from Taxation,	
84	Pounds of Hemp,